God's Daily Promises
for Students

DAILY WISDOM FROM GOD'S WORD

BOOKS IN THE GOD'S DAILY PROMISES SERIES

God's Daily Promises

God's Daily Promises for Women

God's Daily Promises for Men

God's Daily Promises for Students

God's Daily Promises for Leaders

God's Daily

PROMISES

for Students

DAILY WISDOM
FROM GOD'S WORD

Tyndale House Publishers, Inc.

Carol Stream, Illinois

Visit Tyndale's exciting Web site at www.tyndale.com

TYNDALE and Tyndale's quill logo are registered trademarks of Tyndale House Publishers, Inc.

New Living Translation, NLT, and the New Living Translation logo are registered trademarks of Tyndale House Publishers, Inc.

God's Daily Promises for Students: Daily Wisdom from God's Word

General Editors: Ron Beers and Amy Mason

Contributing Editor: Rebecca Beers

Contributing Writers: V. Gilbert Beers, Ronald A. Beers, Brian R. Coffey, Jonathan Farrar, Jonathan Gray, Shawn A. Harrison, Sandy Hull, Rhonda K. O'Brien, Douglas J. Rumford

Designed by Julie Chen

Edited by Michal Needham

ISBN-13: 978-1-4143-1233-0
ISBN-10: 1-4143-1233-4

Printed in the United States of America

13 12 11 10 09 08 07
7   6   5   4   3   2   1

INTRODUCTION

Why did God make so many promises? Maybe it's because he wants to show you how much you can really trust him. Maybe he is so interested in you that he is trying to get your attention with each amazing promise he makes, wanting to show you just how much you have to look forward to as you travel through life. This unique book presents more than 365 of these incredible promises, at least one for every day of the year. All these promises will come true—or have already come true. You simply have to decide whether you want to be part of them or not.

Imagine that every morning you could be inspired by a promise from God's Word and then live the rest of the day with either the expectation that God will fulfill that promise or the confidence that comes from a promise already fulfilled. *God's Daily Promises for Students* is designed to inspire you in just that way. Every page is dated, making the book easy to use. First, read the promise from God. Think about it. Let it soak in. Then read the short devotional note to help you look at your day differently because of God's promise. Finally, read the question at the end to encourage and motivate you to trust that this promise was meant for you. Claim the promise as your own with the confidence that you can always trust God to keep his word. Our prayer is that you will be blessed and encouraged as you see and experience all that God has in store for you.

—*The Editors*

JANUARY

GOALS

TODAY'S PROMISE

All of you should be of one mind, full of sympathy toward each other, loving one another with tender hearts and humble minds. Don't repay evil for evil. Don't retaliate when people say unkind things about you. Instead, pay them back with a blessing. That is what God wants you to do, and he will bless you for it. —1 PETER 3:8-9

TODAY'S THOUGHT

Although it's good to have big goals for personal, academic, or athletic achievements, it's also important to set smaller daily goals. You can determine today to be kind toward others, to be humble, to respond gracefully even when someone takes advantage of you, to read your Bible, to say an encouraging word—these small goals bring great rewards when practiced over a lifetime. God promises to bless you for such small goals of obedience to him, for they become the building blocks of all God wants you to accomplish.

TODAY'S PLAN

What small goals can you set for yourself today?

VALUES

TODAY'S PROMISE

The Holy Spirit produces this kind of fruit in our lives: love, joy, peace, patience, kindness, goodness, faithfulness, gentleness, and self-control.

—GALATIANS 5:22-23

TODAY'S THOUGHT

Godly living means valuing what God values. If you want your values to be the same as God's values, you need God living in you. When you have faith in Jesus, God's Son, he promises to send his Holy Spirit to live within you. The Spirit will help you value what is truly important and then empower you to live it out.

TODAY'S PLAN

Is God's Holy Spirit living within you? Are you allowing him to show you what is really important?

MISTAKES

TODAY'S PROMISE

Oh, what joy for those whose disobedience is forgiven, whose sins are put out of sight. Yes, what joy for those whose record the LORD has cleared of sin.

—ROMANS 4:7-8

TODAY'S THOUGHT

If you've made a mistake and done something wrong, you may not escape the consequences of your actions. But God promises that he can make something good come out of your mistakes and sins if you let him. First confess what you've done wrong, and come clean with God and anyone else you've hurt. Then, through forgiveness and reconciliation, God can make your relationships stronger than they were before. When you mess up, confess it and watch God bring something good out of a bad situation.

TODAY'S PLAN

Are you willing to admit your mistakes so God can bring good out of a bad situation?

WILL OF GOD

TODAY'S PROMISE

Trust in the LORD with all your heart; do not depend on your own understanding. Seek his will in all you do, and he will show you which path to take.

—PROVERBS 3:5-6

TODAY'S THOUGHT

If you walk within God's will today—and every day—you can be sure that you will be walking within his will twenty years from now. God's will for you is to obey him, serve others, read his Word, and do what is right. Do these things and you will never be out of his will. Then when he calls you to do something specific for him, you will be following him close enough to hear his voice and to trust him to lead you.

TODAY'S PLAN

What can you do to follow God's will more closely today?

PRIORITIES

TODAY'S PROMISE

Seek the Kingdom of God above all else, and live righteously, and he will give you everything you need.

—MATTHEW 6:33

TODAY'S THOUGHT

To have the right priorities, you need to have an eternal perspective. That means living today as if you'll be living in heaven tomorrow. It means making choices that will have a greater impact on your eternal life than on your present life. When you develop this eternal perspective, you will realize that what you really need is what God already supplies you with in great abundance. Make serving God your top priority so you can learn what you need to fulfill the purpose and work for which he created you. Make God's Kingdom your primary concern, and what you need will be all about him.

TODAY'S PLAN

How might God meet your needs more abundantly if you changed your priorities?

ACCOUNTABILITY

TODAY'S PROMISE

Young people, it's wonderful to be young! Enjoy every minute of it. Do everything you want to do; take it all in. But remember that you must give an account to God for everything you do.

—ECCLESIASTES 11:9

TODAY'S THOUGHT

God gives you the freedom to follow many different roads and pursue many different activities over the course of your life. He wants you to enjoy everything good that life has to offer. After all, God is the One who created this beautiful world. But he also set boundaries to keep us from abusing our freedom and experiencing the painful consequences of bad choices. Remember that you will have to answer to God for everything you do. You will not be judged for having fun, but you will be judged for enjoying sin. Not everything you do is a call from God, but everything you do is accountable to God.

TODAY'S PLAN

Are you considering any choices that you would eliminate if you had to give an account of your actions to God right now?

CHOICES

TODAY'S PROMISE

Let those who are wise understand these things. Let those with discernment listen carefully. The paths of the LORD are true and right, and righteous people live by walking in them. But in those paths sinners stumble and fall.

—HOSEA 14:9

TODAY'S THOUGHT

Each day we make many choices to follow something. We follow diets, exercise programs, and fashion trends. We follow role models, friends, and other people we admire. We spend our free time following TV shows, sports teams, and entertainment news. But your most important choice is spiritual—will you follow God? Choosing to follow God is a wise choice. He created you and knows what's best for you. When you make the choice to follow God, you can make your other choices in light of God's wisdom and vision for your life.

TODAY'S PLAN

Who or what will you follow today?

BODY

TODAY'S PROMISE

Don't you realize that your body is the temple of the Holy Spirit, who lives in you and was given to you by God? You do not belong to yourself, for God bought you with a high price. So you must honor God with your body. —1 CORINTHIANS 6:19-20

TODAY'S THOUGHT

Your body was made to worship and glorify God and to fulfill the purpose for which he created you. When you do things that are not good for your body or that hurt your body, you are breaking down the very vessel God wants to use to accomplish his work in the world. God works through people, which means he must work through your body to get things done. If you let him, he promises to do great things through you.

TODAY'S PLAN

Are you taking care of your body so God can work through you to do something special?

PLANNING

TODAY'S PROMISE

A prudent person foresees danger and takes precautions. The simpleton goes blindly on and suffers the consequences.
—PROVERBS 22:3

TODAY'S THOUGHT

Planning prepares you for the ups and downs of life. The person who doesn't plan will always be caught off guard by difficult circumstances, but the person who plans ahead will be able to face difficulties with confidence. The most important plans you can make involve how you are preparing yourself for eternity. The way you live now has everything to do with how and where you will live then.

TODAY'S PLAN

What are your plans for eternity? Are you planning to grow in your relationship with God?

HIDING

TODAY'S PROMISE

"Can anyone hide from me in a secret place? Am I not everywhere in all the heavens and earth?" says the LORD.
—JEREMIAH 23:24

TODAY'S THOUGHT

We all hide things from others. Deep in our hearts, there are things we just don't want anyone else to know. Unfortunately, we also try to hide thoughts and feelings from God. We know that it's impossible and even silly, but we do it anyway. Since God knows all the secrets of your heart, why try to hide anything from him? Be honest with God, and tell him about the struggles you have in trying to follow him and live for him. Then you will experience freedom and the full effects of his love.

TODAY'S PLAN

Are you trying to hide something from God?

CALL OF GOD

TODAY'S PROMISE

I knew you before I formed you in your mother's womb. Before you were born I set you apart and appointed you.
                                        —JEREMIAH 1:5

TODAY'S THOUGHT

As a believer, part of your calling is simply to love and obey God. But God may also call you to do something specific for him. When God is calling you to a specific task, he will keep interrupting your thoughts; your heart will long to do what God wants you to do; you will know it is what you should do. Then opportunities will follow to serve him. Seize these moments, and follow God's call. Don't let the window of opportunity close, or you might miss everything God has in store for you.

TODAY'S PLAN

Are you listening for God's call?

SEEKING GOD

TODAY'S PROMISE

Keep on seeking, and you will find. —MATTHEW 7:7

TODAY'S THOUGHT

What or whom you seek out reveals the passions and priorities of your heart. Your chances of accomplishing your goal to find what you seek increase in proportion to the intensity of your commitment. Remarkably, the Bible promises that if you diligently seek the almighty God, you can know and experience him in a personal way. Could you have a loftier goal than that? God desires an intimate and transforming relationship with you. To experience him, you must simply seek him with all your heart.

TODAY'S PLAN

Is God just one of many pursuits for you, or is seeking him your highest goal?

ABSOLUTES

TODAY'S PROMISE

All he does is just and good, and all his commandments are trustworthy. —PSALM 111:7

Every word of God proves true. —PROVERBS 30:5

TODAY'S THOUGHT

If everyone did whatever they wanted, it wouldn't be long before chaos and anarchy would take over. There must be some rules, some laws that people must follow in order for any society to function well. Thus, there must be some absolute truths, set in place from the beginning of time, that apply to all people in all times and all places. God promises that when people live by these absolutes, which are found in his Word, individual lives will function better and society as a whole will be a place of order and peace.

TODAY'S PLAN

Could you make a list of ten absolute truths you should be living by?

REGRETS

TODAY'S PROMISE

Fear not; you will no longer live in shame. Don't be afraid; there is no more disgrace for you. You will no longer remember the shame of your youth. —ISAIAH 54:4

TODAY'S THOUGHT

The past is over. Don't live an "if only" life of regret, feeling angry at yourself for what you have done and bitter toward God for allowing you to do it. God doesn't cause sin or regret or mistakes; he washes them away when you ask him to forgive you and help you move on. Focus on God, who knows your future, not on regret over your past.

TODAY'S PLAN

How do you deal with regret over your past mistakes? Can you forget about them, as God has?

HEROES

TODAY'S PROMISE

The godly people in the land are my true heroes!
I take pleasure in them!
—PSALM 16:3

TODAY'S THOUGHT

Ordinary people become heroes by determining
each day to live for God. God says these people
are his true heroes, and he takes pleasure in
them. It's not what you do that makes you a hero
in God's eyes, it's who you are—a child of God,
committed to doing right and serving him.

TODAY'S PLAN

Are you a hero in God's eyes?

AGE

TODAY'S PROMISE

"O Sovereign LORD," I said, "I can't speak for you! I'm too young!" The LORD replied, "Don't say, 'I'm too young,' for you must go wherever I send you and say whatever I tell you. And don't be afraid of the people, for I will be with you and will protect you. I, the LORD, have spoken!"

—JEREMIAH 1:6-8

TODAY'S THOUGHT

Through God's promise to Jeremiah comes this promise to you: God uses people of all ages to do his work. No one is too young or too old to have an impact for God. People look at outward appearances, including age, but God looks at the heart. And believing hearts come in all ages, from little children to teenagers to grandparents in their golden years.

TODAY'S PLAN

Can you relate to Jeremiah? What might God be calling you to do, even at a young age?

GUIDANCE

TODAY'S PROMISE

You guide me with your counsel, leading me to a glorious destiny.
—PSALM 73:24

TODAY'S THOUGHT

God knows where you've been and what will happen in your future. When you seek his advice, he points you toward places of beauty, joy, and peace, and he helps you avoid the dangerous spots. God promises to be your constant guide on your life's journey, leading you through the dark valleys and up to the mountaintop experiences, finally bringing you to that place of eternal peace and rest you long for.

TODAY'S PLAN

Is God your guide as you travel through life?

DIRECTION

TODAY'S PROMISE

Your word is a lamp to guide my feet and a light for my path. —PSALM 119:105

TODAY'S THOUGHT

The first step to knowing what God wants you to do is getting to know him better. As he communicates to you through his Word, the Bible, he will reveal himself to you and show you which direction to go.

TODAY'S PLAN

Do you read the Bible regularly so you can get to know God better and discover his direction for your life?

WISDOM

TODAY'S PROMISE

My child, listen to what I say, and treasure my commands. Tune your ears to wisdom, and concentrate on understanding. . . . Then you will understand what it means to fear the LORD, and you will gain knowledge of God. . . . Then you will understand what is right, just, and fair, and you will find the right way to go.

—PROVERBS 2:1-2, 5, 9

TODAY'S THOUGHT

Wisdom begins with the understanding that you are accountable to your Creator and fully dependent on him. It's not *what* you know but *who* you know. Wisdom from God helps you develop a biblical outlook that discerns the deceptions and distortions of the world. It helps you apply God's truth and principles to your daily situations and relationships so you know the difference between good and bad, right and wrong.

TODAY'S PLAN

Do you look for wisdom from God or from the world?

POWER OF GOD

TODAY'S PROMISE

We now have this light shining in our hearts, but we ourselves are like fragile clay jars containing this great treasure. This makes it clear that our great power is from God, not from ourselves.

—2 CORINTHIANS 4:7

TODAY'S THOUGHT

God's power can flow through you just like an electric current flows through a wire. The wire is simply a conductor; it has no power by itself. But without the wire, the current doesn't go anywhere. God is looking for people who are willing to be wired for his service. If you are willing to be a conductor of his power, he promises to do amazing things through you.

TODAY'S PLAN

Are you wired for God's service?

TRAINING

TODAY'S PROMISE

Train yourself to be godly. "Physical training is good, but training for godliness is much better, promising benefits in this life and in the life to come."

—1 TIMOTHY 4:7-8

TODAY'S THOUGHT

Training for godliness begins with God's work in you, but then it requires your effort as well. Just as musicians and athletes must develop their talent, strength, endurance, and coordination through intentional effort, Christians must also intentionally train for spiritual fitness. God promises to reward your efforts now and in eternity.

TODAY'S PLAN

How is your training as a Christian progressing? Do you have a spiritual exercise plan?

KNOWLEDGE

TODAY'S PROMISE

These proverbs will give insight to the simple, knowledge and discernment to the young. . . . Fear of the LORD is the foundation of true knowledge.

—PROVERBS 1:4, 7

TODAY'S THOUGHT

The book of Proverbs declares that the fear of the Lord is the foundation of knowledge, meaning that our understanding of the information we receive and the world we live in should pass through the filter of God's wisdom. Knowledge of God and of his rules for living leads to purpose. If you are struggling to find your purpose in life, spend time studying God's Word and getting to know him. He promises to reveal his purposes to you.

TODAY'S PLAN

How well do you know God? Could you know him better? Will you commit to knowing him better, starting today?

ASSIGNMENT

TODAY'S PROMISE

Come, let us go up to the mountain of the LORD, to the house of Jacob's God. There he will teach us his ways, and we will walk in his paths. —ISAIAH 2:3

TODAY'S THOUGHT

You can't just sit around waiting for God to tell you what he wants you to do next; you must be proactive and look for your next assignment. Actively seek God's will by praying, reading the Bible, talking with mature believers and trusted advisers, and paying attention to the people and events God puts in your path. Then God promises that you will see where he wants you to go. For a few people, an assignment from God comes to them in an instant; but for most people, it comes over time as God lays out his direction for you step-by-step.

TODAY'S PLAN

How can you be more proactive in discovering what God wants you to do next?

PLANNING

TODAY'S PROMISE

You can make many plans, but the LORD's purpose will prevail. —PROVERBS 19:21

TODAY'S THOUGHT

Make your plans for each day, but hold them loosely. You can be sure that God will give you new marching orders from time to time, and you must be ready and willing to adjust your own plans when that happens. God's plans for you are always the ones you want to be following.

TODAY'S PLAN

When was the last time God asked you to adjust your plans?

BACKSLIDING

TODAY'S PROMISE

Come back to me and live! —AMOS 5:4

Keep watch and pray, so that you will not give in to temptation. For the spirit is willing, but the body is weak! —MATTHEW 26:41

TODAY'S THOUGHT

It happens to everyone from time to time. You suddenly realize you're further away from God than you should be, and you're worried, even scared. Don't ignore that internal warning! Find out what happened—is it simple neglect or a sinful habit that you don't want to give up? Only when you recognize what you've done can you confess it to God, and only by confessing your sin can you be forgiven and begin the process of restoring your relationship with him.

TODAY'S PLAN

Are you further away from God than you want to be?

WAITING

TODAY'S PROMISE

I wait quietly before God, for my victory comes from him. . . . Let all that I am wait quietly before God, for my hope is in him. . . . O my people, trust in him at all times. Pour out your heart to him, for God is our refuge. —PSALM 62:1, 5, 8

TODAY'S THOUGHT

Sometimes God says yes in answer to your prayers. Sometimes he says no. Often he wants you to wait, because it is through waiting that you can learn the most. Through waiting, you learn to trust God. During times of waiting, you simply have to put your life under God's control, even when you don't understand his ways. Rushing ahead may get you what you think is best, but waiting for God will get God's best for you, and that is always better.

TODAY'S PLAN

How well are you waiting on God?

PRACTICE

TODAY'S PROMISE

Keep putting into practice all you learned and received from me—everything you heard from me and saw me doing. Then the God of peace will be with you.
—PHILIPPIANS 4:9

TODAY'S THOUGHT

Learning to play the piano requires that you first learn the basics and practice them over and over. After you master the basics, you are prepared to learn skills of greater difficulty. Practice is just as important for mastering the basics of the Christian life, for deepening your understanding of God, and for discovering his call on your life. The more you practice spiritual disciplines like prayer, Bible study, and serving others, the more you will grow in spiritual maturity and become the person God created you to be.

TODAY'S PLAN

What spiritual disciplines are you practicing?

POTENTIAL

TODAY'S PROMISE

All glory to God, who is able, through his mighty power at work within us, to accomplish infinitely more than we might ask or think. —EPHESIANS 3:20

TODAY'S THOUGHT

God brings out the best in you, and he sees more in you than you see in yourself. You look at your limitations, but God looks at your potential. If you want a new perspective, learn to see life through God's eyes. He doesn't put nearly as many limitations on you as you put on yourself. He sees you for what he intended you to be as well as for what you are.

TODAY'S PLAN

In what area might God see more potential in you than you see in yourself?

APPEARANCE

TODAY'S PROMISE

Don't be concerned about the outward beauty of fancy hairstyles, expensive jewelry, or beautiful clothes. You should clothe yourselves instead with the beauty that comes from within, the unfading beauty of a gentle and quiet spirit, which is so precious to God.
— 1 PETER 3:3-4

TODAY'S THOUGHT

While it is true that our culture focuses on outward beauty, it is equally true that outward beauty fades and doesn't last. Your physical body is merely a temporary housing for your eternal soul. As a Christian, you will eventually receive a transformed, glorious, eternal body. While it is important to care for your body during your time on earth, you should focus on developing the inward beauty of your spirit. You may not think of yourself as beautiful, but when you develop godliness, others will see the real beauty within you.

TODAY'S PLAN

Are you allowing others to see your inner beauty?

PRESENCE OF GOD

TODAY'S PROMISE

You know when I sit down or stand up. You know my thoughts even when I'm far away. . . . I can never escape from your Spirit! I can never get away from your presence! —PSALM 139:2, 7

TODAY'S THOUGHT

Sometimes you may feel worthless or unlovable or neglected, but you must not let these feelings cause you to withdraw from the One who loves you the most. No matter how you feel, you are never out of God's presence. God can be trusted to keep his promises that he will never leave you or forsake you.

TODAY'S PLAN

When you feel alone, do you push God away or let him draw you close?

DISAPPOINTMENT

TODAY'S PROMISE

They cried out to you and were saved. They trusted in you and were never disgraced. —PSALM 22:5

TODAY'S THOUGHT

You can be sure that God is working in your life to use both the good and the bad for a greater purpose. Nothing that happens to you is completely useless. Disappointment turns into hope as you watch God turn your current troubles into triumphs.

TODAY'S PLAN

How can you see God turning your disappointment into good today?

FEBRUARY

CARE

TODAY'S PROMISE

Give all your worries and cares to God, for he cares about you.
— 1 PETER 5:7

TODAY'S THOUGHT

God's hotline is always open. There is never a busy signal, and he is never too preoccupied— even with managing everything else in the world— to listen to your every need. God promises to offer both a listening ear and a caring heart.

TODAY'S PLAN

How does it feel to know that God cares about what you're going through? Will you share your burdens with him?

DECISIONS

TODAY'S PROMISE

Oh, that we might know the LORD! Let us press on to know him. He will respond to us as surely as the arrival of dawn or the coming of rains in early spring.

—HOSEA 6:3

TODAY'S THOUGHT

Despite the changing nature of the world around you, you can always be secure about two things. First, when you decide that Jesus Christ is the Son of God who died to forgive your sins and rose again so you could live with him forever, you can be absolutely sure that your eternal future is secure in heaven. Second, when you live each day and make each of your decisions based on the changeless truths of God's Word, you will have complete assurance that you are doing the right thing.

TODAY'S PLAN

Are you sure about the decisions you've made on life's most important issues?

PERSISTENCE

TODAY'S PROMISE

The righteous keep moving forward, and those with clean hands become stronger and stronger. —JOB 17:9

TODAY'S THOUGHT

Just because you are following God doesn't make life easy. In fact, the more important the task that God has called you to do, the more roadblocks Satan puts up to stop you. If you know God is leading you in a certain direction, don't give up just because the going gets tough. If anything, such obstacles should tell you that you are headed in the right direction. Keep moving forward boldly with your eyes fixed on God, and he promises that your faith will be strengthened as you persist in doing his will. Then you will be able to step out in faith wherever God calls you.

TODAY'S PLAN

In what area is your life really tough right now? Could it be because you are doing something good for God? How can you find the strength to keep going?

DEPRESSION

TODAY'S PROMISE

From the depths of despair, O LORD, I call for your help.
—PSALM 130:1

TODAY'S THOUGHT

Depression can be serious; it often requires counseling and even medical attention. It also requires spiritual attention. Jesus understands what it feels like to be crushed to the point of despair and to live through what some call "the dark night of the soul." When you feel that low, you may feel hopeless. But the darkness of depression doesn't have to block out the light of God's healing. Seek out all the help you can get, and in the meantime don't forget to cry out to God from your darkness. He will hear you and comfort you, hold you, and begin a work of healing in you.

TODAY'S PLAN

If you're feeling depressed, what step or steps can you take today to find healing, both physically and spiritually?

MATURITY

TODAY'S PROMISE

Let your roots grow down into him, and let your lives be built on him. Then your faith will grow strong in the truth you were taught, and you will overflow with thankfulness.
—COLOSSIANS 2:7

TODAY'S THOUGHT

Reading the Bible and praying to God are the first and most important steps toward spiritual maturity. When your faith is rooted in the Word of God, you will be continually nourished as you soak up the wisdom you read in its pages. When you are committed to talking with God, you will be regularly connecting with the ultimate source of wisdom. You can be sure that you will mature if you stay close to him. As you seek a deeper relationship with God, you will grow stronger and more mature in your faith.

TODAY'S PLAN

Are you looking to the right source to grow in maturity?

GUARDING YOUR HEART

TODAY'S PROMISE

Guard your heart above all else, for it determines the course of your life. —PROVERBS 4:23

TODAY'S THOUGHT

The purpose of a guardrail on a dangerous curve is not to inhibit your freedom to drive but to save your life! In the same way, God has given you a guardrail for traveling through life, not to inhibit your freedom but to keep your life from going out of control. Your heart determines where you go because it affects your passions and emotions. If you don't guard your heart with the boundaries given in the Bible and stay focused on the road God wants you to take, you may have a terrible accident when temptations and sin distract you.

TODAY'S PLAN

What are you doing to guard your heart from temptation?

EXAMPLE

TODAY'S PROMISE

If we love our Christian brothers and sisters, it proves that we have passed from death to life. But a person who has no love is still dead. . . . If someone has enough money to live well and sees a brother or sister in need but shows no compassion—how can God's love be in that person? —1 JOHN 3:14, 17

TODAY'S THOUGHT

Showing love to others is evidence of your relationship with Jesus. Just as a healthy tree produces good fruit, so your life produces good deeds when you have a healthy relationship with Jesus. When you love others no matter what, you become an example to them of God's power and love in your own life. When they see your example, many will recognize that God's Spirit is working through you and will want to know how God can work through them, too.

TODAY'S PLAN

In what way could you be a better example of God's love? Can others see the evidence of your relationship with Jesus?

REPUTATION

TODAY'S PROMISE

Never let loyalty and kindness leave you! Tie them around your neck as a reminder. Write them deep within your heart. Then you will find favor with both God and people, and you will earn a good reputation.
                                                        —PROVERBS 3:3-4

TODAY'S THOUGHT

Everyone has a reputation. Whether you intentionally try to project a certain image or you couldn't care less what others think, people still form an opinion of you based on your personality, your character, your behavior, and your abilities. A good reputation can help you make friends and gain respect. A bad reputation can also help you make friends—the wrong kinds of friends—or it can leave you isolated, shunned, and disrespected. God promises you will earn a good reputation when you show kindness, loyalty, and love to your neighbors.

TODAY'S PLAN

What kind of reputation are you building?

LOVE

TODAY'S PROMISE

Most important of all, continue to show deep love for each other, for love covers a multitude of sins.

—1 PETER 4:8

TODAY'S THOUGHT

What does it mean that "love covers a multitude of sins"? True love is unconditional. No matter what others do to you, regardless of how other people's mistakes hurt you, you love them in return. When others sin against you or hurt you deeply, you don't sin by retaliating. You stop the cycle of sin and hurt. Only love can do that.

TODAY'S PLAN

Whom do you need to respond to in love instead of getting even?

LISTENING

TODAY'S PROMISE

Because he bends down to listen, I will pray as long as I have breath! —PSALM 116:2

TODAY'S THOUGHT

God always listens to your prayers. He never ignores you. Just as you enjoy being with people who really listen to you, you should enjoy spending time with God because he always listens. The more you get to know him, the more you will understand just how much he loves you. Who wouldn't want to talk with someone like that?

TODAY'S PLAN

Do you pray like you believe that God is really listening to you?

REWARDS

TODAY'S PROMISE

No eye has seen, no ear has heard, and no mind has imagined what God has prepared for those who love him.

—1 CORINTHIANS 2:9

TODAY'S THOUGHT

If Christians suffer like everybody else, why bother living for God or following him? If all we had to live for were the rewards of this life, then a "why bother" attitude might be understandable. But this perspective is wrong for at least two reasons. First, when you try to obey God, you end up enjoying life the way it is meant to be enjoyed. Your life displays integrity, and your conscience is clear. Second, this life is not all there is. The Bible is clear that those who trust Jesus Christ for salvation receive the promise of eternal life. Your faithfulness may or may not result in rewards in this life, but your rewards in heaven will be greater than you can imagine.

TODAY'S PLAN

Are you working only for rewards here on earth, or are you looking forward to the rewards God promises in heaven?

APOLOGY

TODAY'S PROMISE

Confess your sins to each other and pray for each other so that you may be healed. —JAMES 5:16

TODAY'S THOUGHT

Saying "I'm sorry" for something you have done wrong is one of the most difficult things to do. You have to recognize your fault, face it head-on, and then humble yourself enough to admit it to someone else. Offering a simple apology demonstrates that you are willing to open the door to healing and blessing. If you want to experience peace and growth in your relationships with friends, loved ones, or God himself, the practice of admitting you are wrong will help you reach a new level of trust and respect with others.

TODAY'S PLAN

Is there someone you need to apologize to? How might your apology help to heal both of you?

CONTENTMENT

TODAY'S PROMISE

Don't love money; be satisfied with what you have. For God has said, "I will never fail you. I will never abandon you." —HEBREWS 13:5

We brought nothing with us when we came into the world, and we can't take anything with us when we leave it. —1 TIMOTHY 6:7

TODAY'S THOUGHT

Contentment comes when you are willing to give up everything for God. It doesn't mean that you *have* to give it all up but that you are *willing* to. Only then are you truly free to relax in the peace and security God offers. Contentment is not about how much you have but what you do for God with what you do have.

TODAY'S PLAN

Is there anything you are not willing to give up for God?

LOVE

TODAY'S PROMISE

There is no greater love than to lay down one's life for one's friends.   —JOHN 15:13

TODAY'S THOUGHT

A healthy definition of love is crucial to understanding the central message of the Bible. According to the Bible, love is not confined to sexuality, nor is it primarily a feeling at all. The Bible teaches that love is a commitment. As such, love does not depend on good feelings but on a consistent and courageous decision to sacrifice oneself for the well-being of another person. That commitment then produces good feelings, not the other way around. Jesus perfectly demonstrated God's unconditional love for us because he gave his life to save us.

TODAY'S PLAN

Think about your own definition of love. Is it based on feelings or commitment?

HEART

TODAY'S PROMISE

Wherever your treasure is, there the desires of your heart will also be.

—LUKE 12:34

TODAY'S THOUGHT

Doctors tell us to exercise and eat right to keep our hearts fit and healthy. In the Bible, the heart is considered to be the center of thought and feeling. It is so important that God cautions you to guard it above all else (see Proverbs 4:23) because your heart filters everything that happens to you and around you. When you neglect your heart, it becomes filthy and clogged with all kinds of foulness—bitterness, jealousy, impure thoughts. A dirty heart can no longer distinguish the good and healthy from the harmful, so it allows hurt and heartache to enter. But when you keep your heart pure and clean, it blocks the toxins of sinful thoughts and desires that could destroy you. A pure heart is the best prescription for a long, happy, and healthy life, and it is essential for living with integrity.

TODAY'S PLAN

When the Great Physician looks at your heart, what condition does he find it in?

ASHAMED

TODAY'S PROMISE

The LORD is my light and my salvation—so why should I be afraid? The LORD is my fortress, protecting me from danger, so why should I tremble?

—PSALM 27:1

TODAY'S THOUGHT

Too often we let the opinions of others paint the picture of our self-worth. Perhaps that's why we might feel ashamed of our faith when others disapprove of it. But your value is determined by God's approval, not the approval or disapproval of others. Your ultimate purpose is to please the God who made you and redeemed you, no matter what others may think of you. When you focus on pleasing God, you won't feel ashamed when others disapprove of your faith.

TODAY'S PLAN

Do you feel ashamed when others disapprove of your faith?

LOYALTY

TODAY'S PROMISE

I no longer call you slaves, because a master doesn't confide in his slaves. Now you are my friends, since I have told you everything the Father told me.

—JOHN 15:15

TODAY'S THOUGHT

Think of the qualities you look for in a friend—honesty, loyalty, and availability, for example. God desires these same qualities in you because you are his friend. He wants you to be honest with him about your struggles and successes, to remain faithful and loyal to him and his Word, and to make yourself available for quality time with him. When you respect, honor, and remain loyal to God, he will call you a friend.

TODAY'S PLAN

Would God call you a loyal friend of his?

COMMITMENT

TODAY'S PROMISE

I have fought the good fight, I have finished the race, and I have remained faithful. And now the prize awaits me—the crown of righteousness, which the Lord, the righteous Judge, will give me on the day of his return.   —2 TIMOTHY 4:7-8

TODAY'S THOUGHT

God doesn't promise that life on earth will be easy, but he does promise to walk with you every step of the way and bring you into glory when he returns. Stay committed to Jesus just as he is committed to you. Keep serving him in whatever he asks you to do. In the end, your commitment will be rewarded, and your reward will exceed all expectation.

TODAY'S PLAN

Do doubts or difficult times make it hard for you to stay strong in your commitment to Jesus? How does today's promise give you hope to endure?

BEST

TODAY'S PROMISE

Work willingly at whatever you do, as though you were working for the Lord rather than for people. Remember that the Lord will give you an inheritance as your reward, and that the Master you are serving is Christ. —COLOSSIANS 3:23-24

TODAY'S THOUGHT

While it may seem overwhelming to give your best in everything for God, this is the kind of attitude that God promises to reward. When you give God your best in your quiet times with him, he will energize you through prayer and his Word. When you give God your best from your material resources, you will be blessed as you see how it can help others. And when you give God your best in serving others, you will be blessed with personal satisfaction as well as deeper relationships. God turns your best efforts into eternal rewards.

TODAY'S PLAN

How can you give your best to God today?

CARE

TODAY'S PROMISE

I will be glad and rejoice in your unfailing love, for you have seen my troubles, and you care about the anguish of my soul. —PSALM 31:7

TODAY'S THOUGHT

God's love and care for you began before you were born, continues throughout your lifetime, and will extend into eternity. Since he created you to have a relationship with him, he cares about every detail of your life. He knows all your troubles and hurts, and he promises to care for you in your suffering.

TODAY'S PLAN

Do you really believe that God cares for you?

DISCOURAGEMENT

TODAY'S PROMISE

Don't be discouraged by this mighty army, for the battle is not yours, but God's. . . . You will not even need to fight. Take your positions; then stand still and watch the LORD's victory.

—2 CHRONICLES 20:15-17

TODAY'S THOUGHT

Do you ever feel like life is a battle and you are on the losing side? When the obstacles in your life seem too big to overcome, it's easy to give in to exhaustion and discouragement. Remember that when you have God on your side, you can tap into his unlimited power. You don't have to win every battle on your own—in fact, God doesn't even want you to. He wants you to ask him for help, and he promises to fight for you.

TODAY'S PLAN

Are you tired and discouraged? Ask God to help you.

HOLINESS

TODAY'S PROMISE

Even before he made the world, God loved us and chose us in Christ to be holy and without fault in his eyes. —EPHESIANS 1:4

Be sure of this: I am with you always, even to the end of the age. —MATTHEW 28:20

TODAY'S THOUGHT

A holy God cannot be in the presence of sin, so how can a sinful person experience God's presence? Only through Jesus Christ's life, death, and resurrection and your faith in him. If you have asked Jesus to forgive your sins, you are now holy and blameless as far as God is concerned. He sees you as if you have never sinned, and he welcomes you into a relationship with him. When you experience this new holiness because of Jesus, you can be sure that God is always with you.

TODAY'S PLAN

Do you believe that you are forgiven and holy in God's eyes? Do you feel like it?

BROKEN HEART

TODAY'S PROMISE

He heals the brokenhearted and bandages their wounds.
—PSALM 147:3

TODAY'S THOUGHT

There is no quick cure for a broken heart. No pill taken twice a day for two weeks will treat it. A broken heart needs a different kind of healing. Generous doses of compassion, listening, love, comfort, encouragement, and blessing will eventually restore joy and hope to your soul. God is the master healer. Other people can help, but no one can touch your broken heart and heal it as God can. When you are hurting, move toward God, not away from him. He is the greatest source of joy and healing.

TODAY'S PLAN

When you are hurting, do you find yourself moving toward God or away from him?

FOLLOWING

TODAY'S PROMISE

If you do not carry your own cross and follow me, you cannot be my disciple. —LUKE 14:27

TODAY'S THOUGHT

Sin often seems fun and enticing, promising "the good life" of pleasure. There is nothing wrong with enjoying good things in life, but when following after pleasure becomes your ultimate goal, it also becomes your god. And since there is no lasting value in pleasure alone, it will eventually leave you feeling bored and empty. Following Jesus puts you on the road to experiencing lasting meaning and purpose. Staying on that road means leaving behind anything that might take your focus off of him and devoting yourself to him with all your heart. Think less about what you are giving up and more about the blessings and benefits of following Jesus.

TODAY'S PLAN

Whom or what are you following?

APPROVAL

TODAY'S PROMISE

Well done, my good and faithful servant. You have been faithful in handling this small amount, so now I will give you many more responsibilities.

—MATTHEW 25:23

TODAY'S THOUGHT

Those who consistently do a good job can usually be trusted with more freedom and responsibility. Their work receives approval from someone who supervises or oversees them. In the same way, the more you serve God, the more he will reward your faithfulness and give you opportunities to serve him with greater freedom and responsibility. Remember that God's love for you never changes, but his approval of your work is based on how well you serve him.

TODAY'S PLAN

Are you ready for God to give you greater freedom and responsibility in serving him?

QUITTING

Let's not get tired of doing what is good. At just the right time we will reap a harvest of blessing if we don't give up.

—GALATIANS 6:9

TODAY'S THOUGHT

When you can see the finish line ahead of you, it's easier to keep going instead of quitting; somehow you can find enough energy to make it to the end. The race of life is no different. Sometimes it seems too long and too hard, and all you want to do is give up. But there is a finish line ahead—heaven. Everyone who crosses the finish line wins and receives rewards beyond imagination. So keep your eyes on heaven, and don't give up when life gets tough!

TODAY'S PLAN

How can you find the energy to keep going when you feel like quitting?

SUFFERING

TODAY'S PROMISE

He has not ignored or belittled the suffering of the needy. He has not turned his back on them, but has listened to their cries for help. —PSALM 22:24

TODAY'S THOUGHT

Suffering is not a sign that there is no God or that God does not love you. Suffering is a fact of life in this fallen world. God is with you in the midst of your struggles. He may not remove them now, but he does promise to help you get through them. And he promises that one day he will take them away. That is why we long for heaven, where there will be no more suffering or the evil that causes it.

TODAY'S PLAN

How can you recognize God's love for you even when you're suffering?

COMMUNICATION

TODAY'S PROMISE

My sheep listen to my voice; I know them, and they follow me.
—JOHN 10:27

TODAY'S THOUGHT

We keep in touch with people because it is vital to the quality and success of our relationships, whether with classmates, friends, family, or spouse. The same principle applies to your relationship with God. You must find ways to communicate with him and learn to listen as he communicates with you. Good communication allows you to experience a breakthrough in your spiritual life. The more time you spend communicating with God, the closer and more successful your relationship with him will be.

TODAY'S PLAN

Are you in touch with God? How much time do you spend communicating with him?

ADDICTION

TODAY'S PROMISE

The Holy Spirit produces this kind of fruit in our lives: love, joy, peace, patience, kindness, goodness, faithfulness, gentleness, and self-control. There is no law against these things! —GALATIANS 5:22-23

TODAY'S THOUGHT

We all have our addictions, whether they are simply bad habits or serious dependencies. One thing all of us are dangerously addicted to is sin. We consistently—daily—disobey God's Word through sinful thoughts, words, or actions. The only cure is to submit to the control of God and his Holy Spirit. When you are under God's control, the Holy Spirit replaces the destructive things in your life with good things. God's transforming power is the only thing that can ultimately heal you of all addictions.

TODAY'S PLAN

What are some fruits of the Spirit you can cultivate today to help break your sin addiction?

MARCH

PERSEVERANCE

TODAY'S PROMISE

I am certain that God, who began the good work within you, will continue his work until it is finally finished on the day when Christ Jesus returns.

—PHILIPPIANS 1:6

TODAY'S THOUGHT

Your ability to persevere is based on the promise of God's persistent, faithful work in your life. God never stops working in you, and that should motivate you to persevere through life. Always be on the lookout for what he will do next to help you grow and serve others.

TODAY'S PLAN

Are you looking forward to what God will do in your life today and tomorrow and the next day? If you can learn to do this, it will be easier to persevere to the end.

MISTAKES

TODAY'S PROMISE

He has removed our sins as far from us as the east is from the west.
                                        —PSALM 103:12

TODAY'S THOUGHT

There can be a big difference between making a mistake and committing a sin. For example, giving the wrong answer on a test is a mistake. Cheating in order to get a better grade is a sin. You can often avoid repeating a mistake by studying harder, planning better, or double-checking your work. But to avoid repeating a sin, you need God's help. The regret you feel over a sin indicates that you want to change your ways. When you confess your sin to God, he promises to change you by removing your sin and completely clearing your record.

TODAY'S PLAN

Have you asked God to forgive you for the sinful mistakes you've made?

ACCEPTANCE

TODAY'S PROMISE

Accept each other just as Christ has accepted you so that God will be given glory. —ROMANS 15:7

TODAY'S THOUGHT

Other people will be greatly influenced by how you treat them, so accept them for who they are. Don't be quick to judge. Don't accept only those people who are like you or who are important or who are popular. Welcome everyone in the way Jesus would welcome them. It isn't a matter of searching out the best people to be around; it's a matter of bringing out the best in the people God has brought to you. Then God will be glorified because the way you treat people will reflect his love and acceptance and will bring out the best in everyone.

TODAY'S PLAN

Do you know someone who does not feel accepted by others? What can you do to affirm and encourage that person?

CIRCUMSTANCES

TODAY'S PROMISE

You suffered along with those who were thrown into jail, and when all you owned was taken from you, you accepted it with joy. You knew there were better things waiting for you that will last forever.

—HEBREWS 10:34

TODAY'S THOUGHT

Accepting your circumstances doesn't necessarily mean liking them. If you keep an eternal perspective, you can learn and grow through difficult times. Accept what comes from God's hand, and trust that he has something to teach you through it. Remember that difficult circumstances will not follow you to heaven. One day there will be no more tears or sorrow. One day God will make everything right.

TODAY'S PLAN

How can you learn to accept the circumstances that come your way?

PANIC

TODAY'S PROMISE

God is our refuge and strength, always ready to help in times of trouble. So we will not fear when earthquakes come and the mountains crumble into the sea.
—PSALM 46:1-2

TODAY'S THOUGHT

Panic makes your heart pound and your mind freeze up. Panic is physically and emotionally paralyzing—worry and fear meet in an instant crisis. You often have no time to prepare for it, and sometimes you're too immobilized by fear to deal with it. If you haven't experienced panic before, or if you haven't prepared for it, you won't be able to deal well with it when it hits. The closer you are to God, your rock of stability, the better you will be able to tap into his courage and peace when panic strikes. Then you will have a clear head so you can act with purpose.

TODAY'S PLAN

Are you close enough to God that you can be at peace when panic strikes?

LAZINESS

TODAY'S PROMISE

Lazy people want much but get little, but those who work hard will prosper.
                                                        —PROVERBS 13:4

TODAY'S THOUGHT

There's a difference between laziness and rest. The Bible says that laziness is a sin, while rest is a reward for hard work. Someday you will be asked to give an account for how you spent your time here on earth. Your responsibility now is to work hard and do well in school, which is often a full-time job in itself. When you've finished your work and done a good job, regularly reward yourself with some much-needed rest. Soon enough you will have to provide for yourself. But don't get lazy—it will hurt you for the rest of your life.

TODAY'S PLAN

What habits of laziness have you been indulging in lately? How can you reward yourself with rest and fun after times of hard work without getting too lazy?

SIGNIFICANCE

TODAY'S PROMISE

*What are people that you should think about them,
mere mortals that you should care for them? Yet
you made them only a little lower than God and
crowned them with glory and honor.* —PSALM 8:4–5

TODAY'S THOUGHT

Deep within every human heart lies a hunger
for significance. We want our lives to count,
to make a difference, to be worth something.
Yet many people carry deep feelings of insig-
nificance. Everywhere they look, they see others who are more successful, more gifted, more
this or that. The Bible says that every person has
great value. You are significant, not because of
anything you can accomplish on your own but
because God created you, cares for you, and
has given you glory and honor.

TODAY'S PLAN

*Do you focus on who you are not or who God created you
to be? Do you focus on what you can't do or what God
can do through you?*

EXPECTATIONS

TODAY'S PROMISE

"My thoughts are nothing like your thoughts," says the LORD. "And my ways are far beyond anything you could imagine."
—ISAIAH 55:8

TODAY'S THOUGHT

God often does the opposite of what we might expect. He chose David, the youngest rather than the oldest son of Jesse, to be king of Israel. He took Saul of Tarsus, the most vicious opponent of the early church, and transformed him into Paul, the greatest missionary of all time. He took the cross, an object of death and ultimate defeat, and made it the sign of victory over sin and death for all eternity. Don't limit God to your own understanding and expectations. He wants to surprise you in ways that inspire your awe, love, gratitude, and joy.

TODAY'S PLAN

In what ways do you expect little from God? How can you expect more than you dreamed possible?

PRAYER

TODAY'S PROMISE

If my people who are called by my name will humble themselves and pray and seek my face and turn from their wicked ways, I will hear from heaven and will forgive their sins.
— 2 CHRONICLES 7:14

TODAY'S THOUGHT

Prayer is having a conversation with God. It takes humility to talk to God and admit that you need his help. It takes humility to admit that you don't have all the answers and you can't control everything that happens to you. But as a believer, you have the privilege of being able to talk with God—telling him your thoughts and feelings, praising him, thanking him, confessing your sin, asking for his help and advice, and listening for his answers. The essence of prayer is humbly entering into the very presence of almighty God. When you do, he promises to listen and answer.

TODAY'S PLAN

How do you approach God in prayer—humbly seeking him or glibly ticking off a list of requests?

CHALLENGES

TODAY'S PROMISE

Dear brothers and sisters, when troubles come your way, consider it an opportunity for great joy. For you know that when your faith is tested, your endurance has a chance to grow. So let it grow, for when your endurance is fully developed, you will be perfect and complete, needing nothing. —JAMES 1:2-4

TODAY'S THOUGHT

Just as it takes the rough surface of a file to sharpen and smooth the blade of a knife, so it takes rough times to sharpen you into the kind of person God can effectively use. Any challenge can be a tool that God will use to make you sharper, bringing you greater wisdom to persevere, maturity to withstand the hard knocks, and the ability to overcome life's obstacles with courage and grace. As you endure challenges, you will gain confidence to face whatever comes your way.

TODAY'S PLAN

How might God be sharpening you right now? Let him use these rough times to perfect your faith.

WITNESSING

TODAY'S PROMISE

When you are brought to trial in the synagogues and before rulers and authorities, don't worry about how to defend yourself or what to say, for the Holy Spirit will teach you at that time what needs to be said.

—LUKE 12:11-12

TODAY'S THOUGHT

Even the boldest witnesses find themselves in situations where it is difficult or even dangerous to share their faith. God promises that you can call on him for courage to speak the truth confidently, and he will give you the right words to speak. The effectiveness of God's message does not depend on the eloquence of your own speech but on the power of the living God communicating through you. God is the One who touches people's hearts, and he promises to do so through the words of willing witnesses.

TODAY'S PLAN

The next time you need to speak up and give witness of your faith, can you trust God to speak through you?

HAPPINESS

TODAY'S PROMISE

Those who look to him for help will be radiant with joy. . . . Taste and see that the LORD is good. Oh, the joys of those who take refuge in him!

—PSALM 34:5, 8

TODAY'S THOUGHT

Happiness is often a temporary feeling, a reaction to happy events. But joy is a strong and lasting state of being. You can have joy despite your circumstances. Happiness resulting from your circumstances is fine and good, but if that's all you can count on, you will have to continually seek out happy events to keep the good feelings going. On the other hand, people who have the joy that comes from God don't need good times to keep them happy. They learn how to develop inner joy in spite of their circumstances. They know that no matter what happens, God offers them eternal hope and always keeps his promises.

TODAY'S PLAN

Do you spend more time pursuing happiness or joy?

GOODNESS

TODAY'S PROMISE

*"I know the plans I have for you," says the LORD.
"They are plans for good and not for disaster, to give
you a future and a hope."* —JEREMIAH 29:11

TODAY'S THOUGHT

Many people picture God as stern and vindictive, just watching and waiting for the chance to zap humans with bolts of misfortune. But this verse shows the opposite. God loves you and wants only good things for you. He wants your future—both in this life and in heaven—to be bright and hopeful.

TODAY'S PLAN

*How can you begin to recognize God's goodness all
around you?*

JUDGMENT

TODAY'S PROMISE

Since we have been made right in God's sight by the blood of Christ, he will certainly save us from God's condemnation. For since our friendship with God was restored by the death of his Son while we were still his enemies, we will certainly be saved through the life of his Son. —ROMANS 5:9-10

TODAY'S THOUGHT

Because we like to be in control, one of the hardest things to accept is that we don't make the rules for how life and faith work—God does. God's rules say that sin deserves eternal death, and everyone has sinned. Your assurance for salvation is based on the fact that Jesus Christ stood in your place and took the judgment you deserved for your sin. God promises that he no longer judges you as an enemy but as a friend—even his own child.

TODAY'S PLAN

Have you accepted Jesus' sacrifice so you won't have to face eternal judgment?

ENERGY

TODAY'S PROMISE

I pray that from his glorious, unlimited resources he will empower you with inner strength through his Spirit.
—EPHESIANS 3:16

TODAY'S THOUGHT

The Holy Spirit lives in every believer, and with him comes the power of God. When you give control of your life to the Holy Spirit, he releases his power within you—power to resist temptation, to serve and love God and other people even when you are at the end of your rope, to have wisdom in all circumstances, and to persevere in living for God today with the promise of eternal life someday. Through his Spirit, God will give you the energy you need to do everything he asks you to do.

TODAY'S PLAN

Are you allowing God's Holy Spirit to bring God's power into your life?

POWER OF GOD

TODAY'S PROMISE

Do not let sin control the way you live; do not give in to sinful desires. . . . Instead, give yourselves completely to God, for you were dead, but now you have new life. So use your whole body as an instrument to do what is right for the glory of God. Sin is no longer your master, for you no longer live under the requirements of the law. Instead, you live under the freedom of God's grace.
—ROMANS 6:12-14

TODAY'S THOUGHT

One of Satan's biggest lies is that you are a victim—you have no power to resist the temptations that surround you. The world teaches you that heredity, environment, or circumstances are to blame for your actions. But God is more powerful than anything else that seeks to control you. When you call on his power, God breaks the chains of sin and sets you free.

TODAY'S PLAN

Are you tapping into God's power so you can be free from sin?

MARCH 17

PATIENCE

You are my strength; I wait for you to rescue me, for you, O God, are my fortress. —PSALM 59:9

TODAY'S THOUGHT

The best way to develop patience is to exercise it. God sometimes makes you wait because he wants you to learn to trust him in the meantime. God will give you answers when he's ready, and when he is ready, the timing will be best for you, too. Your time on hold is not wasted if you are serving God right where you are. Just trust that God's timing is better than your own.

TODAY'S PLAN

Is God asking you to wait patiently for something right now?

DECISIONS

TODAY'S PROMISE

Believe in the Lord Jesus and you will be saved.

—ACTS 16:31

TODAY'S THOUGHT

The most important decision you will ever make is whether or not you will follow the one true God. This decision requires you to believe that his Son, Jesus, died on the cross for your sins and rose from the dead so that you can have a relationship with him. When you make this decision, God promises that you will live forever with him in heaven.

TODAY'S PLAN

Have you made life's most important decision?

SALVATION

TODAY'S PROMISE

If you confess with your mouth that Jesus is Lord and believe in your heart that God raised him from the dead, you will be saved. —ROMANS 10:9

TODAY'S THOUGHT

If you believe that Jesus saves you, if you confess your sins to him and receive his forgiveness, and if you acknowledge that he is Lord of your life, then he makes you a new person inside. You have received salvation, meaning God has saved you from the punishment you deserve for your sins and instead gives you eternal life with him in heaven. There is no sweeter deal! Sin no longer controls you. Although your relationship with Jesus begins at a particular moment, you should maintain an active, daily faith in Jesus Christ that continues throughout your life, giving you the power and hope to overcome your problems and troubles until you reach heaven.

TODAY'S PLAN

Do you have God's salvation?

RESPECT

TODAY'S PROMISE

All honor and glory to God forever and ever! He is the eternal King, the unseen one who never dies; he alone is God. Amen.
—1 TIMOTHY 1:17

TODAY'S THOUGHT

Too often we treat God as ordinary, forgetting that he is completely holy and all-powerful. We must be extremely careful to treat God with the reverence he deserves. Thinking of him as Santa Claus or the man upstairs is disrespect-ful, and so is using his name to swear or spice up your language. If you treat God as ordinary, it shows that you do not understand who he is or what he can do. Respect for God means that you show reverence for his name. The One who designed and created the universe deserves and demands our respect.

TODAY'S PLAN

In what ways do you treat God as ordinary? How can you show him the respect he deserves?

RENEWAL

TODAY'S PROMISE

*Put on your new nature, and be renewed as you
learn to know your Creator and become like him.*

—COLOSSIANS 3:10

TODAY'S THOUGHT

Most of us have to admit that we are not who
we really want to be. We're not as disciplined,
thoughtful, productive, loving, or caring as we
would like. And sometimes our lives need more
than just a little tinkering—we need a fresh start.
When you become a follower of Jesus, he promises renewal that will bring you peace, joy, and
a whole new perspective on life. Jesus offers to
redeem your thoughts, attitudes, habits, regrets,
and relationships. You can become the person
God wants you to be and who you want to be
as well.

TODAY'S PLAN

What part of your life most needs God's renewal?

GOALS

We can make our plans, but the LORD determines our steps.
— PROVERBS 16:9

When a ship sets out on a long voyage at sea, the captain needs to plot the course. This includes choosing the route, setting the schedule, determining the places to stop, and deciding the responsibilities for each crew member. By planning ahead and setting attainable goals, the captain ensures that the ship will stay on the right track and arrive safely at its destination. The same principle is true for you. Setting attainable goals is necessary for determining your destination and your course for getting there. Without goals, you would wander aimlessly through life. When you allow God to be your captain and plot your life's journey according to his plan for you, then you will stay on track and arrive safely at your ultimate destination—heaven.

How can you align your goals with God's direction for your life?

TRUTH

TODAY'S PROMISE

We will not be influenced when people try to trick us with lies so clever they sound like the truth. Instead, we will speak the truth in love, growing in every way more and more like Christ, who is the head of his body, the church. —EPHESIANS 4:14-15

TODAY'S THOUGHT

Human desires are fickle and constantly changing. That's why you should focus on becoming more like Christ and on what he wants for you. The truth is, you often don't know what is best for you, or even what is true or false. The only way to know the truth is to continually study what the God of truth says in his Word, the Bible. Reading and studying the Bible is one of the ways God works in your life to make you more like Christ and to reveal whatever he has in store for you.

TODAY'S PLAN

Are you learning truth from the God of truth?

DOUBT

TODAY'S PROMISE

We proclaim to you the one who existed from the beginning, whom we have heard and seen. We saw him with our own eyes and touched him with our own hands. He is the Word of life. This one who is life itself was revealed to us, and we have seen him. And now we testify and proclaim to you that he is the one who is eternal life.

—1 JOHN 1:1-2

TODAY'S THOUGHT

The resurrected Jesus Christ was seen by count-less credible witnesses. The disciples were trans-formed from doubters to courageous witnesses who could not be silenced. The truth of Jesus' claim to be God's Son was validated by his resurrection. If God can bring Jesus back from the dead, you should have no doubts about any of the other wonderful things he promises to those who believe in him.

TODAY'S PLAN

Do you believe that God can transform your doubt into confident faith?

SUFFERING

TODAY'S PROMISE

Dear friends, don't be surprised at the fiery trials you are going through, as if something strange were happening to you. Instead, be very glad—for these trials make you partners with Christ in his suffering, so that you will have the wonderful joy of seeing his glory when it is revealed to all the world.

—1 PETER 4:12-13

TODAY'S THOUGHT

Suffering helps you better understand what Jesus went through for you. Jesus suffered cruelty and death to give you the greatest gifts of all—salvation and eternal life. So you should joyfully suffer for him, if need be, and faithfully proclaim his message despite the suffering it might cause you. When you suffer for Jesus, you appreciate so much more the way that he suffered for you.

TODAY'S PLAN

Have you had to suffer for your faith in Jesus? Are you willing to?

HEAVEN

TODAY'S PROMISE

Jesus told [Thomas], "I am the way, the truth, and the life. No one can come to the Father except through me." —JOHN 14:6

TODAY'S THOUGHT

Jesus is the only way to heaven. You may want to buy your way in, work your way in, or think your way in. But the Bible is clear—Jesus Christ is the only way in. He is not being intolerant; he is providing you with the secret to eternal life! Believing and gratefully accepting this truth is the only way to get to life's most important destination.

TODAY'S PLAN

Do you believe that Jesus is the only way to heaven?

FREEDOM

TODAY'S PROMISE

Look, today I am giving you the choice between a blessing and a curse! You will be blessed if you obey the commands of the LORD your God that I am giving you today. But you will be cursed if you reject the commands of the LORD your God.

—DEUTERONOMY 11:26-28

TODAY'S THOUGHT

It sounds contradictory, but evil exists because God is loving. The Bible teaches that God created human beings with the freedom to choose—either to love and obey him and do what is right, or to disobey him and do what is wrong. God gave us this gift of freedom because without it, there can be no love. God could have created us so that we could only do good—thus eliminating the possibility of evil—but then we would be robots without the capacity to choose or to love. Only when you have freedom to choose does love become real.

TODAY'S PLAN

With your God-given freedom of choice, have you chosen God?

RESURRECTION

TODAY'S PROMISE

The angel spoke to the women. "Don't be afraid!" he said. "I know you are looking for Jesus, who was crucified. He isn't here! He is risen from the dead, just as he said would happen. Come, see where his body was lying." —MATTHEW 28:5-6

TODAY'S THOUGHT

The resurrection of Jesus, the greatest event in human history, is the foundation of the hope that you have as a Christian. Jesus promised that he would rise from the dead, and because he did, you can be sure that he has power over death and that his promise to give you eternal life will come true. His resurrection is the beginning of eternal life for everyone who believes in him. Do you believe?

TODAY'S PLAN

Do you believe that Jesus has power over death and that he will resurrect you for eternal life with him?

SIGNIFICANCE

TODAY'S PROMISE

*O LORD, you . . . know everything about me. . . .
You know everything I do. . . . Such knowledge is
too wonderful for me, too great for me to understand!*

—PSALM 139:1-3, 6

TODAY'S THOUGHT

You may feel that you disappear into the crowd,
but you are not invisible to God. He created
you for relationship with him, and that gives
you significance. No one else is like you or can
do what God created you to do. This makes you
extremely valuable to him. When you stay close to
God, you will be able to feel his love and discover
his purpose for your life.

TODAY'S PLAN

*As you walk through the crowds today, remember that
you are significant because you are valued by God.*

RESURRECTION

TODAY'S PROMISE

It's not that we want to die and get rid of these bodies that clothe us. Rather, we want to put on our new bodies so that these dying bodies will be swallowed up by life. God himself has prepared us for this, and as a guarantee he has given us his Holy Spirit. —2 CORINTHIANS 5:4-5

TODAY'S THOUGHT

Your resurrected body will be a physical body like you have now, but it will also have supernatural characteristics. You may be able to walk through walls, as Jesus did with his resurrected body. Your new body won't age or decay from the effects of sin. You will never be sick or injured again, and your mind will never think sinful thoughts. When you believe that this is true and live like you believe it, you will be able to look forward to the final resurrection and also inspire those around you.

TODAY'S PLAN

Are you living each day with the confidence that you will be resurrected on the last day?

ASSUMPTIONS

Don't just say to each other, "We're safe."

—MATTHEW 3:9

There is only one God, and he makes people right with himself only by faith, whether they are Jews or Gentiles.

—ROMANS 3:30

TODAY'S THOUGHT

Don't just assume you will go to heaven. The Bible says the only way to heaven is through faith in Jesus Christ, God's Son. When you believe in the truth of Jesus' life, death, and resurrection, you are able to have a relationship with God. He sends the Holy Spirit to live within you to help you live out your faith and produce spiritual fruit. You then have the assurance—not just the assumption—that you belong to God and will spend eternity with him in heaven.

TODAY'S PLAN

Are you certain that you're going to heaven?

APRIL

COMMITMENT

My child, . . . never let loyalty and kindness leave you! Tie them around your neck as a reminder. Write them deep within your heart. Then you will find favor with both God and people.

—PROVERBS 3:1-4

TODAY'S THOUGHT

If you aren't really committed to God, you can fool people for a while, but who you are on the inside will ultimately show itself on the outside. Your words and actions will eventually reflect your heart. For example, attending worship regularly shows your commitment to putting God first in your heart. Being kind shows your commitment to serving others. God promises that when your heart's first commitment is to know and love him, then you will gain a good reputation with others and with God.

TODAY'S PLAN

What is your heart most committed to? If you aren't sure, then others probably aren't either.

CHANGE

TODAY'S PROMISE

Anyone who belongs to Christ has become a new person. The old life is gone; a new life has begun!

—2 CORINTHIANS 5:17

TODAY'S THOUGHT

Change is one of the great constants of life. The Bible teaches two great truths about change. The first is that despite the changing world around us, God is changeless and dependable. The second is that God requires an inner change of heart, called repentance, that produces an outward change of lifestyle, called obedience. When your heart is changed, your life will be changed forever.

TODAY'S PLAN

Have the unchanging truths of Scripture changed your heart and life?

CONFESSION

Everyone who believes in [Jesus] will have their sins forgiven through his name. —ACTS 10:43

Confession is the act of recognizing that you have done something wrong, that it has hurt your relationship with God, and that you want his forgiveness. Confession indicates your desire to get back in a right relationship with God. There are two kinds of confession. When you first ask Jesus to forgive your sins and you acknowledge him as your Lord and Savior, you are given the gift of salvation. That is a once-in-a-lifetime event. But after you are saved, you need to regularly confess your sins before Jesus. Sin can still separate you from him, and confession releases the power of God's forgiveness and restores your relationship with him.

Do you need to confess any sins in order to restore your relationship with Jesus?

TEMPTATION

Guard your heart; do not be unfaithful to your wife.

—MALACHI 2:16

You have heard the commandment that says, "You must not commit adultery." But I say, anyone who even looks at a woman with lust has already committed adultery with her in his heart.

—MATTHEW 5:27-28

TODAY'S THOUGHT

Temptation often begins with the eyes and travels quickly to the heart. What you do immediately after you see something or someone that poses a temptation for you will affect your thoughts and actions beyond the situation at hand. If you let your eyes linger where they shouldn't, your mind will follow and will find ways to justify your gaze. Then your heart will start tugging you in that direction. The first step in avoiding temptation is taking your eyes off whatever may be tempting you.

TODAY'S PLAN

How can you protect your eyes from whatever tempts you?

IMAGINATION

TODAY'S PROMISE

Listen to me, all who hope for deliverance—all who seek the LORD! . . . The LORD will comfort Israel again and have pity on her ruins. Her desert will blossom like Eden, her barren wilderness like the garden of the LORD. Joy and gladness will be found there. Songs of thanksgiving will fill the air.

—ISAIAH 51:1-3

TODAY'S THOUGHT

Use your imagination to make God's promises of new life and eternal life come alive in your mind. Someday, when God transforms this earth into a new one, he promises to turn the deserts into lush land like the Garden of Eden. Not only will barren places become fertile, but the curse of sin will be gone. Imagine life without the curse, and have faith that it will happen. Then your relationship with God will grow even stronger.

TODAY'S PLAN

Imagine a world free from the curse of sin. What do you see yourself doing there?

WORSHIP

TODAY'S PROMISE

I will meditate on your majestic, glorious splendor and your wonderful miracles. . . . The LORD is close to all who call on him, yes, to all who call on him in truth. —PSALM 145:5, 18

TODAY'S THOUGHT

You are already in God's presence, but if you need help feeling God's presence, begin by worshiping him. Approach him with gladness. Sing a song to him in your heart. Praise and thank him for what he has done for you and for others. Pause to notice the beauty of his creation that you see all around you. This will make you more aware of God's presence—in moments of peace, in acts of kindness, and in the strength that he provides to help you through tough times.

TODAY'S PLAN

Do you wait to worship God until you feel his presence? How can you be proactive about initiating times of worship?

FORGIVENESS

TODAY'S PROMISE

If we confess our sins to him, he is faithful and just to forgive us our sins and to cleanse us from all wickedness.

—1 JOHN 1:9

TODAY'S THOUGHT

God forgives your sin when you ask him. After he forgives you, he looks at you as though you have never sinned. A holy and pure God cannot be in the presence of the contamination of sin, so you must be washed clean of sin before you can come into his presence. Forgiveness scrubs away the sin so you can be restored to purity in God's eyes.

TODAY'S PLAN

Do you ask for God's forgiveness so you can be restored to him?

SACRIFICE

TODAY'S PROMISE

Who can list the glorious miracles of the LORD?
Who can ever praise him enough? —PSALM 106:2

Let us offer through Jesus a continual sacrifice of
praise to God, proclaiming our allegiance to his
name. —HEBREWS 13:15

TODAY'S THOUGHT

You can thank God by offering him a sacrifice
of praise. What does that mean? It means that
you sacrifice something, or give up something,
in order to praise him. You might give up some
of your sleep to get up early to praise him. Maybe
you could give up some of your free time to pray
and worship. Perhaps you need to give up
complaining so you can praise him for all
he has done for you. Whatever your sacrifice might be, give it up to give God praise.

TODAY'S PLAN

Think of the sacrifice God made to have a relationship
with you; what does that inspire you to sacrifice in order
to grow in your relationship with him?

GRACE

TODAY'S PROMISE

The LORD is compassionate and merciful, slow to get angry and filled with unfailing love. —PSALM 103:8

TODAY'S THOUGHT

Your beliefs about God are more important than any other beliefs you have. If you believe that God is always angry with you, you will likely be defensive, fearful, or antagonistic toward him. But when you believe that God shows you deep love and grace, you can live in the joy of being forgiven and knowing you will live forever in heaven with him. You will no longer fear God's retribution but will thank him for his grace.

TODAY'S PLAN

Do you believe in a God who is full of anger or grace?

RESURRECTION

TODAY'S PROMISE

Christ lives within you, so even though your body will die because of sin, the Spirit gives you life because you have been made right with God. The Spirit of God, who raised Jesus from the dead, lives in you. And just as God raised Christ Jesus from the dead, he will give life to your mortal bodies by this same Spirit living within you. —ROMANS 8:10-11

TODAY'S THOUGHT

Jesus' resurrection was the essential aspect of God's plan to allow you to spend eternity with him. Because Jesus was raised from the dead, you can be sure that he has power over death and that you, too, will be resurrected one day to live forever with God in heaven. If Jesus had not defeated death, there would be no hope for eternal life. The fact that he did is the central message and purpose of the Good News of Jesus.

TODAY'S PLAN

Is belief in Jesus' resurrection—and yours—the central part of your faith?

LOVE

TODAY'S PROMISE

Let's not get tired of doing what is good. At just the right time we will reap a harvest of blessing if we don't give up. Therefore, whenever we have the opportunity, we should do good to everyone—especially to those in the family of faith.
—GALATIANS 6:9-10

TODAY'S THOUGHT

It's easy to like people who are likable, but you model God's love more when you show love to those who are unlovable. There are no perfect people—even among Christians. But you can take joy in reaching out to and loving those imperfect people God has placed in your sphere of influence. You may be surprised at how God can bring the most unlikely individuals together as friends. When you reach out to others in love, your heart will be changed.

TODAY'S PLAN

Who in your life is difficult to love? How can you show love for that person anyway?

GENEROSITY

TODAY'S PROMISE

The same Lord . . . gives generously to all who call on him. —ROMANS 10:12

TODAY'S THOUGHT

God has generously offered you the gift of life forever in a perfect world. All you have to do is accept and believe that he's really giving you such a magnificent gift. If God were not a generous and compassionate God, he might require his followers to work for their salvation, or he might give only a privileged few the chance to get into heaven. But God is generous, and he offers the same gift to everyone who comes to him.

TODAY'S PLAN

Have you accepted the generous gift God is offering you?

WISDOM

TODAY'S PROMISE

If you keep yourself pure, you will be a special utensil for honorable use. Your life will be clean, and you will be ready for the Master to use you for every good work. —2 TIMOTHY 2:21

TODAY'S THOUGHT

How can you make wise decisions at a moment's notice? The key is to be prepared by developing wisdom over time. One way you do that is by keeping yourself pure—filling your mind with God's Word instead of the world's advice. You can't anticipate everything that might happen today, but when you are prepared spiritually— when you have developed godly wisdom—you will know the right thing to do so God can use you to accomplish good. You will be ready to act swiftly and decisively because you have a wellspring of wisdom to draw upon.

TODAY'S PLAN

How does keeping yourself pure increase God's wisdom in your life?

HEAVEN

TODAY'S PROMISE

Look, God's home is now among his people! He will live with them, and they will be his people. God himself will be with them. He will wipe every tear from their eyes, and there will be no more death or sorrow or crying or pain. All these things are gone forever. —REVELATION 21:3-4

TODAY'S THOUGHT

Eternity is not just an extension of life here on earth, where we suffer, grieve, and hurt. God will restore this earth to the way he once created it—a beautiful place without sin, sorrow, or pain. The new earth will have similarities to this one, but it will be better and more amazing in every way. You will be in God's presence, forever filled with joy.

TODAY'S PLAN

What in this life makes you long for heaven?

APRIL 15

MEANING

*My life is worth nothing to me unless I use it for
finishing the work assigned me by the Lord Jesus.*

—ACTS 20:24

*I take joy in doing your will, my God, for your
instructions are written on my heart.* —PSALM 40:8

TODAY'S THOUGHT

You don't need to do earthshaking things in
order to have a meaningful life. Your life has
meaning when you do the work that God has
given you to do. Whether you are doing homework, hanging out with friends, working a part-
time job, or going on a mission trip, when you
do it to please God, do it as though God is
working through you—he is! Your life has
meaning because you are sharing the love
of God with everyone in your circle of
influence.

TODAY'S PLAN

How can you find meaning in your activities today?

CHURCH

TODAY'S PROMISE

Where two or three gather together as my followers, I am there among them.　　　　—MATTHEW 18:20

TODAY'S THOUGHT

God lives in the heart of every believer, but he also lives within the community of the church. When the church is gathered together, God meets his people in a special way. Just as being present at a live concert or sports event makes it much more exciting, participating with other believers in worshiping God makes it much more meaningful. Together you experience the presence and power of God in ways you never could on your own.

TODAY'S PLAN

How can you experience God more deeply with other believers?

HOPE

TODAY'S PROMISE

The hopes of the godly result in happiness, but the expectations of the wicked come to nothing.

—PROVERBS 10:28

TODAY'S THOUGHT

Ultimately, there is no greater happiness than knowing you will live with God forever in the perfect world of heaven. No matter how hope-less things seem now, you can have joy in your heart as you focus on eternity. Because you believe in Jesus, you have real, eternal hope. People who don't know Jesus Christ have no hope beyond this life. But he promises a joyful, eternal future in heaven to those who know him, and that promise brings you hope.

TODAY'S PLAN

Does your hope of heaven affect the way you live now?

ASSURANCE

TODAY'S PROMISE

Those the Father has given me will come to me, and I will never reject them. —JOHN 6:37

TODAY'S THOUGHT

Your assurance is rooted in God's hold on you, not your grip on God. When you give your life to him, he will hold you and never let go. You can approach God knowing that he will always welcome you and never reject you. He will never say, "Sorry, I don't have time for you" or "Don't bother me." You can be assured that God always listens, always responds, always loves, always is there for you.

TODAY'S PLAN

How can you live today with the assurance of God's love?

FAIRNESS

The wages of sin is death, but the free gift of God is eternal life through Christ Jesus our Lord.

—ROMANS 6:23

Let us fall into the hands of the LORD, for his mercy is great.

—2 SAMUEL 24:14

Don't be too quick to beg God for justice, because he might have to punish you because of your sin. Instead, beg God for his love so he will forgive you. Don't be too quick to beg God for fairness, because he might end up taking away what you have. Instead, beg God for mercy so you can be saved from the judgment that all people deserve. Because of Christ, God's idea of fairness allows him to grant mercy to those whose hearts sincerely love him.

Would you rather have complete fairness now or experience God's mercy for eternity?

HEAVEN

TODAY'S PROMISE

Let me reveal to you a wonderful secret. We will not all die, but we will all be transformed! . . . For our dying bodies must be transformed into bodies that will never die; our mortal bodies must be transformed into immortal bodies.

—1 CORINTHIANS 15:51-53

TODAY'S THOUGHT

One day you will be like Jesus. You will not be equal to him in power and authority, but you will be like him in character and perfection, for there will be no sin in heaven. You will never again experience pain or sorrow, and evil will be gone forever.

TODAY'S PLAN

How does your hope of heaven help you live better today?

APATHY

Anyone who isn't with me opposes me, and anyone who isn't working with me is actually working against me. —MATTHEW 12:30

TODAY'S THOUGHT

Apathy can cause you to lose what you want the most. If you are apathetic about a friendship, you are in danger of losing that friend. If you are apathetic about saving money, you will not have much later on. If you are apathetic toward God, you are in danger of losing the priceless rewards that await his followers in heaven. Apathy often seems to be a passive force that simply lulls you to sleep, but it can also be an aggressive force that prevents you from keeping what is most meaningful and important.

TODAY'S PLAN

Are you in danger of losing something or someone important to you? How can you protect yourself from the dangers of apathy?

TEMPTATION

TODAY'S PROMISE

The temptations in your life are no different from what others experience. And God is faithful. He will not allow the temptation to be more than you can stand. When you are tempted, he will show you a way out so that you can endure.

—1 CORINTHIANS 10:13

TODAY'S THOUGHT

Don't underestimate the power of Satan, but don't overestimate it either. He can tempt you, but he cannot force you to sin. He can dangle the bait in front of you, but he cannot make you take it. The Bible promises that no temptation will ever be too strong for you to resist. Even in times of overwhelming temptation, God provides you with a way out. In those times, the Holy Spirit gives you the power and the wisdom to find a way to escape.

TODAY'S PLAN

What temptation do you need an escape from?

DIVERSITY

TODAY'S PROMISE

The human body has many parts, but the many parts make up one whole body. So it is with the body of Christ. . . . If the ear says, "I am not part of the body because I am not an eye," would that make it any less a part of the body? If the whole body were an eye, how would you hear? . . . But our bodies have many parts, and God has put each part just where he wants it.

—1 CORINTHIANS 12:12-18

TODAY'S THOUGHT

The apostle Paul likens the body of Christ to the human body, in which every part has its own specific function. It doesn't make sense to try to figure out whether your hand or your foot is more impor-tant—you need both. God promises that when everyone works together, his Kingdom will grow and flourish! The more you appreciate the diversity within the body of Christ, the more you will be able to accomplish together for the glory of God.

TODAY'S PLAN

How can you accept and even celebrate the diversity you see among those you worship with?

OPPORTUNITIES

TODAY'S PROMISE

Make the most of every opportunity in these evil days.
—EPHESIANS 5:16

We must quickly carry out the tasks assigned us by the one who sent us. The night is coming, and then no one can work.
—JOHN 9:4

TODAY'S THOUGHT

God regularly places divine appointments right in front of you—opportunities to do good, to help someone in need, or to share what you know about God. Always be on the lookout for these opportunities to witness to your faith through words or actions. God will put the opportunities in front of you, but you need to act on them. God promises that he will make the most of your act of faith.

TODAY'S PLAN

How can you be more aware of the opportunities for witnessing that God will put in front of you today?

APRIL 25

HOLY SPIRIT

TODAY'S PROMISE

He generously poured out the Spirit upon us through Jesus Christ our Savior. —TITUS 3:6

TODAY'S THOUGHT

One of God's most generous gifts is that he provides his Holy Spirit to all who believe in him. God doesn't give this gift just to the ultra-righteous or giants of the faith. He gives his presence in the form of the Holy Spirit to everyone who believes in his Son, Jesus, who is the only way to heaven and eternal life with him. The Holy Spirit encourages you to live for God, keeps your focus on heaven, and protects you from attacks by the enemy.

TODAY'S PLAN

Are you using God's gift of the Holy Spirit to help you on your life's journey?

LONELINESS

TODAY'S PROMISE

Nothing can ever separate us from God's love. Neither death nor life, neither angels nor demons, neither our fears for today nor our worries about tomorrow—not even the powers of hell can separate us from God's love. No power in the sky above or in the earth below—indeed, nothing in all creation will ever be able to separate us from the love of God. —ROMANS 8:38-39

TODAY'S THOUGHT

Do you ever wrestle with feelings of loneliness? Do you ever feel rejected? Perhaps your best friend deserted you. Or your parents are getting divorced. You don't feel any less alone on a crowded city street or in a busy airport. But God's promise to the lonely is, "Do not be afraid, for I am with you" (Isaiah 43:5). In addition to his presence, God promises to love you no matter what.

TODAY'S PLAN

Do you feel God's presence and his love even when you are all alone?

SHARING

TODAY'S PROMISE

When Christ, who is your life, is revealed to the whole world, you will share in all his glory. —COLOSSIANS 3:4

TODAY'S THOUGHT

Ever since we were little children, we've been taught to share. Yet for most of us, it remains as hard as ever to share either our things or ourselves. Why? Because at the very core of our sinful human nature is the desire to get, not give; to accumulate, not relinquish; to look out for ourselves, not for others. The Bible calls you to share many things—your resources, your faith, your love, your time, your talents, your money. It promises that those who share generously will discover the benefits of giving, which are far greater than the temporary satisfaction of receiving. God was willing to share his own Son with you so that you could have eternal life. When you realize how much God has shared with you, you will be more willing to share with others to bless their lives.

TODAY'S PLAN

What do you have that you can share generously with others?

HYPOCRISY

If someone claims, "I know God," but doesn't obey God's commandments, that person is a liar and is not living in the truth. But those who obey God's word truly show how completely they love him.

—1 JOHN 2:4-5

TODAY'S THOUGHT

If you confess your sins but don't change your behavior, you're living a spiritual charade. It's hypocrisy to deliberately continue in sin, but it's easy to glibly ask God for forgiveness with no real desire to change your behavior. God promises that if you are sincere about confessing your sins, he will be sincere about forgiving you. But if you seek forgiveness only as an afterthought or as a way to get yourself off the hook, God will see through you. Only a changed life is a sure sign of your sincerity and God's forgiveness.

TODAY'S PLAN

Which do you want more—to be forgiven or to avoid punishment? Your answer shows whether you have a hypocritical attitude.

MONEY

TODAY'S PROMISE

Trust in your money and down you go!

—PROVERBS 11:28

TODAY'S THOUGHT

The way you handle your money reveals the condition of your soul. If Jesus asked you to, could you give up your favorite things? Could you ride the city buses, move to a crowded apartment in a poor neighborhood, get your clothes secondhand, and buy food at the local food bank—if that's how Jesus wanted you to serve him? Your response to questions like these may show you whether money is your servant or your master. The best way to handle money is to regularly test how much you trust in it by seeing how much of it you can give away.

TODAY'S PLAN

What does today's thought reveal to you about the importance of money in your life?

ATTITUDE

TODAY'S PROMISE

If you are suffering in a manner that pleases God, keep on doing what is right, and trust your lives to the God who created you, for he will never fail you.

—1 PETER 4:19

TODAY'S THOUGHT

Problems, trials, troubles, and the testing of your faith can either strengthen your resolve or wear you down—it all depends on your attitude. If you see your problems as stepping-stones to something greater, then you can move ahead with anticipation for what you will become— a person of strong character who can handle any obstacle. If you see your problems as insurmountable barriers, you will get discouraged, give up, and turn back, preventing yourself from becoming more than you are now. God promises that suffering can help you grow if you let him work in you.

TODAY'S PLAN

How do you see your problems? Are you in need of an attitude adjustment?

MAY

MODESTY

TODAY'S PROMISE

Be careful to live properly among your unbelieving neighbors. Then even if they accuse you of doing wrong, they will see your honorable behavior, and they will give honor to God when he judges the world. —1 PETER 2:12

TODAY'S THOUGHT

Modesty means maintaining godly standards of appropriate dress and behavior that keep you from being a stumbling block to others. It means keeping your appearance in harmony with the faith, love, and holiness you profess as a believer. Modesty frees you from focusing excessive time and attention on yourself and worrying about how you appear to others. When you don't give others the chance to question your outward appearance, they will be better able to focus on what's inside of you—a heart that loves Jesus.

TODAY'S PLAN

Have you thought about how your outward appearance might distract people from seeing the beauty of God in your heart?

POTENTIAL

TODAY'S PROMISE

I pray that your hearts will be flooded with light so that you can understand the confident hope he has given to those he called—his holy people who are his rich and glorious inheritance. —EPHESIANS 1:18

TODAY'S THOUGHT

You can begin to develop your spiritual potential when you recognize the damaging potential of your sinful nature. The Bible promises that when you give Jesus control of your life, the Holy Spirit comes into your heart. The Spirit then begins the work of helping you reach the spiritual potential for which you were created— to become more like Christ and to use your spiritual gifts to help others. If you are not following Christ, you cannot live up to the potential God created within you.

TODAY'S PLAN

What might God be able to do in you if you gave yourself completely to him?

ABILITIES

TODAY'S PROMISE

In his grace, God has given us different gifts for doing certain things well. —ROMANS 12:6

TODAY'S THOUGHT

The natural abilities you have are gifts from God, and they are often a clue to what God wants you to do. Would God give you certain talents and abilities, and then not ask you to use them? You may have natural gifts in the area of sports, music, art, academics, leadership, helping oth-ers, or any number of other areas. Use whatever gifts you have been given to bring honor and glory to God. Then you will be right where you need to be to accomplish the purpose for which he created you.

TODAY'S PLAN

Make a list of some of your natural abilities. Are you making good use of them?

GOD'S WORD

TODAY'S PROMISE

The word of God is alive and powerful. It is sharper than the sharpest two-edged sword, cutting between soul and spirit, between joint and marrow. It exposes our innermost thoughts and desires. —HEBREWS 4:12

TODAY'S THOUGHT

God's Word is the light that brings you face-to-face with the darkness of sin overshadowing your heart. Just as light extinguishes darkness, God's Word shines into the dark corners of your life, revealing your sins so that you can extinguish them through confession and forgiveness. Only when you stop hiding your sins can you be released from their power to control you. Keep the light of God's Word in your heart so there will be no dark areas for sin to live in.

TODAY'S PLAN

Are you prepared to let God's Word reveal your hidden sins?

ANGER

TODAY'S PROMISE

Stop being angry! Turn from your rage! Do not lose your temper—it only leads to harm. —PSALM 37:8

TODAY'S THOUGHT

Anger is often a reaction to your pride being hurt. When you are confronted, rejected, ignored, or don't get your own way, anger acts as a defense mechanism to protect your ego. It is common to feel angry when someone confronts you about your own sinful actions because you don't want others to think you have done something wrong. But the Bible promises that anger—unless it is righteous anger—will always bring harm.

TODAY'S PLAN

What kinds of things cause you to get angry?

IMPOSSIBILITY

TODAY'S PROMISE

Jesus looked at them intently and said, "Humanly speaking, it is impossible. But with God everything is possible."   —MATTHEW 19:26

TODAY'S THOUGHT

You need faith in order to experience the impossible and recognize it for what it is. Faith gives you the new perspective that what you see is not all there is. You are able to recognize the impossible things God does for his people when you believe that anything is possible for him. Learn to recognize and appreciate those impossible things God does for you and around you each day—even something as obvious as giving and sustaining life. The more you see the impossible acts of God with eyes of faith, the stronger your faith will become.

TODAY'S PLAN

Look for all the impossible things that God will make possible today. How many can you find?

LISTENING

TODAY'S PROMISE

If you listen to correction, you grow in understanding.
                                        —PROVERBS 15:32

TODAY'S THOUGHT

Listening involves being open to advice. To grow in understanding, you must be willing to accept correction when you make mistakes. When you listen to advice, you should absorb it both with your mind and with your heart. Then it will come in handy at just the right time, when you are most vulnerable to temptation and need understanding to fight against it.

TODAY'S PLAN

Are you open to advice? What piece of godly advice have you received in the past that has really stuck with you?

CREATION

TODAY'S PROMISE

It is the LORD who provides the sun to light the day and the moon and stars to light the night, and who stirs the sea into roaring waves. His name is the LORD of Heaven's Armies. —JEREMIAH 31:35

Whatever is good and perfect comes down to us from God our Father, who created all the lights in the heavens. He never changes. —JAMES 1:17

TODAY'S THOUGHT

Who but the Creator can control creation? All of creation is a testimony to the powerful hand of God. The facts of creation—that the sun comes up and warms you, that the rain waters the land, that the seasons continue without fail— reveal a God who still holds the world in his loving and powerful hands.

TODAY'S PLAN

How can you let the wonders of creation remind you of the Creator?

SELF-CONTROL

TODAY'S PROMISE

How can a young person stay pure? By obeying your word.
—PSALM 119:9

TODAY'S THOUGHT

Self-control involves knowing God's guidelines for living, which are found in the Bible. You need to know what you must control before you can succeed at controlling it. Regularly and consistently reading God's Word will keep his guidelines clearly before you. God's Word will guide and empower you to obey his commands; his promises will awaken hope within you; and his counsel will give you wisdom and direction.

TODAY'S PLAN

How can God's Word help you develop your self-control?

THOUGHTS

TODAY'S PROMISE

Fix your thoughts on what is true, and honorable, and right, and pure, and lovely, and admirable. Think about things that are excellent and worthy of praise. . . . Then the God of peace will be with you.

—PHILIPPIANS 4:8-9

TODAY'S THOUGHT

Make an effort to practice thinking good thoughts, just as you might practice doing some other skill. Such thoughts might be about the good things in your life that you can be thankful for, the good in others that you appreciate, the good deeds that you could do for others, or the goodness of God in providing you with earthly blessings and the promise of eternal life.

God promises that when you think good thoughts, your heart will be at peace.

TODAY'S PLAN

What good things can you spend more time thinking about?

TIME

TODAY'S PROMISE

Teach us to realize the brevity of life, so that we may grow in wisdom.　　　　　　　—PSALM 90:12

TODAY'S THOUGHT

Believe it or not, the best way to find more time is to devote more time to worshiping God and to resting yourself. Devoting time to God gives you spiritual refreshment and the opportunity to discover his priorities for you. Devoting time to rest gives you physical refreshment and the energy to do what God calls you to do. When you make more time for these two activities, you will find more purpose and meaning in what you do, and you will have enough time to do everything you need to do.

TODAY'S PLAN

Are you spending enough time with God to know how he wants you to use your time?

HOLINESS

I, the LORD, am holy, and I make you holy.

—LEVITICUS 21:8

TODAY'S THOUGHT

Holiness means that you reflect God's nature in every way. The word *holy* comes from a word that means "to be separate" or "to be set apart." As such, holiness includes not only your moral integrity but also your entire outlook on life as you realize that you are in the world but not of it. God is the only one who can make you holy. He promises to help you break free from the sinful attractions of this world so that you can live for him and really make a difference.

TODAY'S PLAN

Do you have a holy outlook on life?

LIMITATIONS

TODAY'S PROMISE

I can do everything through Christ, who gives me strength. —PHILIPPIANS 4:13

TODAY'S THOUGHT

When you doubt God's ability to perform a miracle or to change an impossible situation in your life, you are putting limitations on an almighty God. God can accomplish more than you could ever dare to hope for, so don't limit him by your disbelief. Nothing is impossible for him. He can help you get rid of bad habits, sinful thoughts and desires, or anything else that might keep you from experiencing his love and freedom. God promises to give you unlimited blessings when you simply believe and say, "I can do everything with the help of Christ!"

TODAY'S PLAN

What limitations might you be placing on God?

PERFECTION

TODAY'S PROMISE

Our High Priest offered himself to God as a single sacrifice for sins, good for all time. . . . For by that one offering he forever made perfect those who are being made holy.
—HEBREWS 10:12-14

TODAY'S THOUGHT

Many of us strive for perfection. We want to be the perfect friend, perform flawlessly in school, or be super skilled at a particular sport or hobby. Here on earth we will always be struggling against the reality of our humanness and sinful nature, which stand in the way of our quest for perfection. What we are really longing for is heaven, where perfection is the norm. Jesus was perfect, holy, and blameless. Through his death on the cross, he exchanges our human sinfulness for his perfect holiness. Now we are blameless before God, and he promises that one day we will be perfect in heaven.

TODAY'S PLAN

Can you imagine God seeing you as perfect? He does, if you've asked him to forgive and save you. Can you imagine being perfect? You will be one day in heaven.

GODLINESS

TODAY'S PROMISE

Oh, the joys of those who do not follow the advice of the wicked, or stand around with sinners, or join in with mockers. But they delight in the law of the LORD, meditating on it day and night. They are like trees planted along the riverbank, bearing fruit each season. Their leaves never wither, and they prosper in all they do. —PSALM 1:1-3

TODAY'S THOUGHT

The Bible uses metaphors of trees and vines and fruit to paint a picture of what a godly life should look like. As God's follower, you are to live a life that bears the fruit of goodness, justice, kindness, love, and truth, which are important and productive means of cultivating God's Kingdom on earth. When others see your godliness, they will be drawn to the beauty of his way of living.

TODAY'S PLAN

When others look at you, do they see the beauty of your faith and godly living?

COUNTERCULTURAL

TODAY'S PROMISE

The world would love you as one of its own if you belonged to it, but you are no longer part of the world. . . . Since they persecuted me, naturally they will persecute you. And if they had listened to me, they would listen to you. They will do all this to you because of me, for they have rejected the One who sent me. —JOHN 15:19-21

TODAY'S THOUGHT

If you follow Jesus rather than the world, you will be misunderstood, possibly even mocked and persecuted. God's message is countercultural. When you follow his ways—for example, pray for your enemies or give away your money to help others—it will not make sense according to today's cultural standards. As a result, you can expect some ridicule and opposition. But that won't always be the norm. In God's new culture in heaven, goodness and righteousness will be the norm.

TODAY'S PLAN

Is the way you live each day countercultural?

SEXUAL SIN

TODAY'S PROMISE

God's will is for you to be holy, so stay away from all sexual sin. Then each of you will control his own body and live in holiness and honor—not in lustful passion like the pagans who do not know God and his ways. —1 THESSALONIANS 4:3-5

TODAY'S THOUGHT

The world tells us, "If it feels good, do it!" But sin often feels good, so good feelings don't make something right or good. God says that within a marriage relationship, sex is special and sacred, a holy act that symbolizes your faithfulness to God and your intimacy with him. God also says that outside of marriage, sex trivializes and degrades what is holy. God says that sexual sin damages you spiritually. When you become a Christian, you dedicate yourself wholly to the Lord, and that includes your body. Don't damage it physically or spiritually through sexual sin.

TODAY'S PLAN

Are you caring for your body and your soul by avoiding sexual sin?

CHRISTLIKENESS

TODAY'S PROMISE

All of us who have had that veil removed can see and reflect the glory of the Lord. And the Lord— who is the Spirit—makes us more and more like him as we are changed into his glorious image.

—2 CORINTHIANS 3:18

TODAY'S THOUGHT

The more time that two people spend together, the more alike they become. They adopt certain figures of speech or accents of the other person. They sometimes begin to dress alike or even think alike. The same is true when you spend more and more time with Jesus. Soon your speech becomes gentle and kind, your face mirrors his joy, your attitudes and motives become more pure, and your actions become more focused on serving others. When Christ changes you, it's always for the better!

TODAY'S PLAN

Can other people see you becoming more and more like Jesus every day?

CHRISTLIKENESS

TODAY'S PROMISE

It is no longer I who live, but Christ lives in me. So I live in this earthly body by trusting in the Son of God, who loved me and gave himself for me.

—GALATIANS 2:20

TODAY'S THOUGHT

Don't simply ask for things from God; ask him to make you be like him. He has given you the amazing promise that you can become more like him and do much of what he has done because Christ is in you.

TODAY'S PLAN

Are you becoming more like Jesus?

CHARACTER

TODAY'S PROMISE

Supplement your faith with a generous provision of moral excellence, and moral excellence with . . . love for everyone. The more you grow like this, the more productive and useful you will be in your knowledge of our Lord Jesus Christ.   —2 PETER 1:5-8

TODAY'S THOUGHT

Character is what you are, but it is also what you want to become. If you are striving for good character—better yet, for godly character—you are working toward moral excellence. Think of all the areas in your life, such as school or hobbies, in which you've worked hard to develop excellence. Doesn't it also make sense to work hard at becoming morally excellent, mastering the things that really matter, such as integrity, kindness, love, and faithfulness?

TODAY'S PLAN

Your reputation, or what other people say about you, is often a good measure of your character. If you could hear others talking about you, what might they be saying?

STABILITY

TODAY'S PROMISE

He alone is my rock and my salvation, my fortress where I will never be shaken. —PSALM 62:2

TODAY'S THOUGHT

Can you lose everything and still have stability in your life? God promises that you can answer yes to this question. He gives you clear principles for finding true stability. Unlike the weather or interest rates, God never changes, so you know his promises always come true. If you cling only to the stability that this world offers, you will be unsteady and can be shaken by the troubles that will come your way. But if you embrace the eternal and unchanging God, you will stand firm and unshakable throughout your life.

TODAY'S PLAN

What if you lost everything that is most important to you? Do you have the eternal stability that comes from knowing God?

HOPE

Faith is the confidence that what we hope for will actually happen; it gives us assurance about things we cannot see. —HEBREWS 11:1

We were given this hope when we were saved. (If we already have something, we don't need to hope for it.) —ROMANS 8:24

TODAY'S THOUGHT

Hope means expecting something that has not yet occurred. Once hope is fulfilled, it isn't hope anymore. Thus, an important part of hope is waiting patiently for God to work. As you exercise your faith that God will do what he has promised, you also become absolutely sure that he will. Your hopes are not idle hopes because they are built on the solid foundation of God's trustworthiness.

TODAY'S PLAN

Which of God's promises has he already fulfilled in your life, and which do you still hope for?

PATIENCE

TODAY'S PROMISE

Put your hope in the LORD. Travel steadily along his path. He will honor you. —PSALM 37:34

TODAY'S THOUGHT

Patience comes from trusting God day by day to help you on life's journey. It's easier to be patient when you are making steady progress. God promises to give you the strength to travel steadily on the path he has laid out for you. Your patience will grow as you see yourself making small steps forward each day.

TODAY'S PLAN

What small step of faith can you take today?

ENTHUSIASM

TODAY'S PROMISE

The seed on the rocky soil represents those who hear the message and immediately receive it with joy. But since they don't have deep roots, they don't last long. They fall away as soon as they have problems or are persecuted for believing God's word.

—MATTHEW 13:20-21

TODAY'S THOUGHT

When you get serious about your faith, your enthusiasm for God grows by leaps and bounds. To keep from being shallow, read God's Word daily, study it, avoid temptation, and learn to recognize Satan's traps. Don't let your enthusiasm for following God fade, or you will be in danger of falling away from your faith.

TODAY'S PLAN

What dampens your enthusiasm for Jesus? How can you guard against it?

PRAYER

TODAY'S PROMISE

The eyes of the Lord watch over those who do right, and his ears are open to their prayers. But the Lord turns his face against those who do evil. —1 PETER 3:12

TODAY'S THOUGHT

God not only listens carefully to every prayer, he also answers each one. God may answer yes, no, or wait, just as loving parents might answer the request of their child with one of these three responses. Answering yes to every request would spoil you and endanger your well-being. Answering no to every request would be vindictive, stingy, and hard on your spirit. Answering wait to every request would frustrate you. God always answers your prayers according to what he knows is best for you. When you don't get the answer you want, you will grow in spiritual maturity as you seek to understand why God's answer is in your best interest.

TODAY'S PLAN

What are some things you've prayed about but haven't received the answer you want? How might God's answer be best for you?

CREATION

By faith we understand that the entire universe was formed at God's command, that what we now see did not come from anything that can be seen.

—HEBREWS 11:3

TODAY'S THOUGHT

The Bible is clear that God made the universe by his command. You did not happen by chance but by the design of a loving Creator. Even when you are uncertain about why things happen, you can be absolutely sure about God's presence and his plan and purpose—for you and for all of creation.

TODAY'S PLAN

How can creation make you more certain of God's presence in your life?

TEMPTATION

TODAY'S PROMISE

The Lord is faithful; he will strengthen you and guard you from the evil one. —2 THESSALONIANS 3:3

TODAY'S THOUGHT

The Bible teaches that one of Satan's main goals is to tempt you to sin—although your own selfish appetites certainly make the tempter's work easier. Just as blood attracts a shark, so your weaknesses attract Satan's attacks. The key is to identify where you are most vulnerable—where you have the greatest tendency to sin. Then ask God to strengthen you in those areas. He promises to help you fight and endure the temptations when Satan attacks you again.

TODAY'S PLAN

In what area of your life are you most tempted to do wrong? How can God strengthen you in that area?

PLEASURE

TODAY'S PROMISE

You will show me the way of life, granting me the joy of your presence and the pleasures of living with you forever. —PSALM 16:11

TODAY'S THOUGHT

God created you to find pleasure in your relationship with him. The pleasures and blessings that come from knowing him are the most wonderful aspects of the Christian life. Try finding pleasure in God; ultimately that will give you more pleasure than the earthly, physical pleasures God also wants to bless you with.

TODAY'S PLAN

Do you believe that God wants to limit your pleasure or increase it?

COMPROMISE

TODAY'S PROMISE

Be very careful never to make a treaty with the people who live in the land where you are going. If you do, you will follow their evil ways and be trapped. —EXODUS 34:12

TODAY'S THOUGHT

This seems like a strange promise, but it points out the danger of falling into a lifestyle of sin. The laws of society make you pay a fine or go to prison when you commit a crime because of the recognition that certain behaviors harm others. If those behaviors are left unchecked, rebellion and chaos will reign. That is why God warns you not to compromise with the evil that surrounds you. If you do, you will soon be living comfortably with sin rather than struggling to be true to God and his Word.

TODAY'S PLAN

How can you live in today's culture without compromising your convictions?

CHARACTER

TODAY'S PROMISE

*We can rejoice, too, when we run into problems
and trials, for we know that they help us develop
endurance. And endurance develops strength of
character, and character strengthens our confident
hope of salvation.*
                                                    —ROMANS 5:3-4

TODAY'S THOUGHT

As you mature in your faith, you will become
stronger. This inner strength will give you wisdom beyond your years and spiritual power to
help you accomplish more than you ever thought
possible. As your character develops, your confidence in your salvation increases and the assurance of God's love fills your soul.

TODAY'S PLAN

*How has your character been tested lately? Did it
strengthen your confidence in God's love and salvation?*

FEAR

TODAY'S PROMISE

He will cover you with his feathers. He will shelter you with his wings. His faithful promises are your armor and protection. Do not be afraid of the terrors of the night, nor the arrow that flies in the day. Do not dread the disease that stalks in darkness, nor the disaster that strikes at midday. —PSALM 91:4-6

TODAY'S THOUGHT

When your problems and obstacles consume you, you often give in to fear—fear that you will fail, fear that you will let others down, fear that God will not help you when you need it most. Fear tempts you to focus on the size of your problem rather than on the size of your God. Focus on God in faith, and you will sense him fighting by your side to overcome the obstacles in front of you.

TODAY'S PLAN

What are you most afraid of? Is what you fear bigger than God?

JUNE

RESTLESSNESS

The LORD said . . . "This vision is for a future time. . . . If it seems slow in coming, wait patiently, for it will surely take place. It will not be delayed."

—HABAKKUK 2:2-3

Sometimes we lose patience with God. We become restless and bored while we wait for his plans to be fulfilled in our lives. Patiently waiting for God can actually help you anticipate each new day. God is doing what is best for you, so his plan will be accomplished on his schedule, not yours. Keeping that in mind, you can actually become excited about waiting for him to act. You awake each day anticipating what good thing he will accomplish in your life, and it will be just right for you at just the right time.

When you start to feel restless, how can you change your attitude so you can look forward to whatever God is about to do in your life?

FOLLOWING

TODAY'S PROMISE

Jesus called out to them, "Come, follow me, and I will show you how to fish for people!" And they left their nets at once and followed him. —MATTHEW 4:19-20

TODAY'S THOUGHT

Jesus' invitation to follow him remains a mere opportunity until you decide to accept it. He requires a decision: Follow him or remain where you are. Accepting his invitation leads to action. The disciples stopped what they were doing and followed Jesus. God extends his invitation to you, too.

TODAY'S PLAN

Have you accepted Jesus' invitation to follow him?

FEAR OF GOD

TODAY'S PROMISE

Don't be afraid, for I am with you. Don't be discouraged, for I am your God. I will strengthen you and help you. I will hold you up with my victorious right hand. —ISAIAH 41:10

TODAY'S THOUGHT

Usually we think of fear as an unpleasant emotion tied to anxious worry or outright terror of being harmed. But there is another definition of fear that leads to something good and wonderful. Fear of God means having complete awe and respect for him, realizing that everything he says about love and justice is true. Because God is great and mighty and holds the power of life and death in his hands, a healthy, reverent fear of him helps us respond to him as we should. This actually draws us closer to him and the blessings he gives.

TODAY'S PLAN

How do you respond to God's greatness and might?

CONFUSION

TODAY'S PROMISE

The LORD directs our steps, so why try to understand everything along the way? —PROVERBS 20:24

TODAY'S THOUGHT

Life is less confusing when you realize and accept that God truly is in control. The purpose of God's control is not to manipulate you or order you around but to assure you that this world is not random and chaotic. If that were the case, life would be meaningless. But because God is in control of the world, you can be sure his promises will come true. You can live a life of purpose rather than confusion and make a difference for all eternity. How wonderful to know that when you are confused, God has the answer!

TODAY'S PLAN

What are you confused about? How does knowing that God is in control help you deal with it?

GIVING UP

TODAY'S PROMISE

Think of all the hostility [Jesus] endured from sinful people; then you won't become weary and give up. . . . So take a new grip with your tired hands and strengthen your weak knees. —HEBREWS 12:3, 12

TODAY'S THOUGHT

When you are tempted to give up, remember the endurance Jesus displayed during his earthly life. Though he was fully divine, Jesus was also fully human. He felt hungry, sad, and tired. He looked to his Father for help and found the strength to keep going and fulfill his mission here on earth. That same strength is available to you if you seek it.

TODAY'S PLAN

Before you give up, can you find the energy to go to God for help?

JUNE 6

ACCOMPLISHMENTS

TODAY'S PROMISE

With God's help we will do mighty things.

—PSALM 60:12

TODAY'S THOUGHT

At the most basic level, to accomplish something
means to complete a task, whether it is finishing
your homework or leading your team to victory.
The Bible describes many tangible accomplishments, but it also highlights many spiritual
accomplishments, which we so often overlook.
A spiritual accomplishment might be having an
active prayer life, maturing in the faith, telling a
classmate about Jesus, gaining victory over temptation, offering a word of encouragement. God
promises that these kinds of accomplishments
do the greatest good and bring the greatest
rewards.

TODAY'S PLAN

What will you try to accomplish today?

CRITICISM

TODAY'S PROMISE

Do not judge others, and you will not be judged. For you will be treated as you treat others. The standard you use in judging is the standard by which you will be judged. —MATTHEW 7:1-2

TODAY'S THOUGHT

When you criticize others and have no intent to see them succeed or improve, you are judging them. This kind of criticism not only reveals a word problem but also a heart problem. On the other hand, constructive criticism is giving advice in a gentle and loving way, investing in others for the purpose of building them up and helping them become who God created them to be. Before criticizing someone else, take stock of your own sins and shortcomings so that you can approach that person with understanding and humility.

TODAY'S PLAN

What things do you criticize or judge others for? Examine your heart and ask God to help you approach people more lovingly.

MERCY

TODAY'S PROMISE

God blesses those who are merciful, for they will be shown mercy.   —MATTHEW 5:7

TODAY'S THOUGHT

One of the hardest things to do is to forgive someone who has wronged you. But it is only through forgiveness that you can be freed from bitterness. The mercy you show to someone may be exactly what that person needs to understand and accept God's mercy. God promises that the blessings of mercy will return to those who show mercy to others.

TODAY'S PLAN

Do you need to show mercy to someone today?

TRUTH

TODAY'S PROMISE

Jesus said to the people who believed in him, "You are truly my disciples if you remain faithful to my teachings. And you will know the truth, and the truth will set you free." —JOHN 8:31-32

TODAY'S THOUGHT

Truth sets people free from ignorance and deception. Since God is truth, he sets the standard for truth. Knowing God's standards for living frees you from the ignorance and deception of what the world claims is true.

TODAY'S PLAN

How well do you know God's truth? Have you ever been deceived by what the world says is true?

SALVATION

TODAY'S PROMISE

I am not ashamed of this Good News about Christ. It is the power of God at work, saving everyone who believes. . . . This Good News tells us how God makes us right in his sight. This is accomplished from start to finish by faith. —ROMANS 1:16–17

TODAY'S THOUGHT

God offers everyone the most amazing gift— freedom from eternal death to enjoy life with him forever in heaven, where all is good and perfect. It sounds too good to be true, but that is the Good News. All you have to do is believe it by accepting the truth that Jesus died for your sins. When you do, your guilt is completely taken away. Your life is so changed that you'll grate- fully follow Jesus and live his way, because anyone who can free you from a death sen- tence is worth following. God wants you to enjoy your freedom and make the most of it.

TODAY'S PLAN

Have you accepted the gift of God's salvation?

CONFIDENCE

TODAY'S PROMISE

Dear friends, we are already God's children, but he has not yet shown us what we will be like when Christ appears. But we do know that we will be like him, for we will see him as he really is. —1 JOHN 3:2

TODAY'S THOUGHT

Confidence comes from the realization and assurance that God loves you, that he has given you specific talents and gifts, that he wants you to use those gifts for him, and that he has given you salvation and eternal life in heaven. Knowing these truths gives you complete confidence that your life has meaning now and into eternity.

TODAY'S PLAN

How can you live with meaning and purpose today because of your confidence in God's promises?

OBEDIENCE

TODAY'S PROMISE

The LORD God is our sun and our shield. He gives us grace and glory. The LORD will withhold no good thing from those who do what is right.

—PSALM 84:11

TODAY'S THOUGHT

Since God is the Creator of life, he knows how life is supposed to work. Even though God's commandments are sometimes difficult to follow or don't make sense from a human perspective, obedience to them will always bring blessing, joy, and peace. Obedience demonstrates that you are willing to trust God and follow through on what he says is best for you. Obedience is the visible expression of your love.

TODAY'S PLAN

Do you see obedience as the pathway to blessing?

VALUE

TODAY'S PROMISE

Don't rob the poor just because you can, or exploit the needy in court. For the LORD is their defender. He will ruin anyone who ruins them.

—PROVERBS 22:22-23

TODAY'S THOUGHT

What's the difference between paper plates and fine china? Value. Paper plates are used once and then thrown into the trash, but fine china is kept for generations and treated with the utmost care. We place a higher value on fine china than we do on paper goods. When we use other people or take advantage of them, we're treating them like paper plates—worthless and disposable. But the Bible tells us that all people have lasting value—so much more than fine china. Each person is a special creation with a special purpose and deserves to be treated with the utmost respect and care.

TODAY'S PLAN

Do you have the courage to ask your closest friends to hold you accountable when you take advantage of others instead of valuing them?

SIN

TODAY'S PROMISE

He personally carried our sins in his own body on the cross so that we can be dead to sin and live for what is right. By his wounds you are healed. —1 PETER 2:24

TODAY'S THOUGHT

If there were no consequences for driving through red lights, breaking into people's homes, or killing people, anarchy would reign. The things societies value most—peace, order, security—would be gone. Sin is breaking the laws that the Creator of the universe gave us to bring peace, order, and security to our world. Breaking God's laws brings God's punishment, just as breaking civil laws brings civil punishment. The good news is this: When Jesus died on the cross, he took the punishment for sin that you deserve. Sin no longer controls you. God gives you the power to overcome sin and live according to his laws until the day when there will be no more sin.

TODAY'S PLAN

Do you consistently break any of God's laws? Could this be the cause of disorder or insecurity in your life?

PAIN

TODAY'S PROMISE

I will be glad and rejoice in your unfailing love, for you have seen my troubles, and you care about the anguish of my soul. —PSALM 31:7

He will wipe every tear from their eyes, and there will be no more death or sorrow or crying or pain. All these things are gone forever. —REVELATION 21:4

TODAY'S THOUGHT

We've all experienced the debilitating feeling of an ill or wounded body or the ache of a broken heart. Your greatest hope in times of pain is to find healing in God. Although he does not promise to remove your pain in this life, he does promise to be with you in it and give you hope and purpose despite your hurting body and soul. Most importantly, God promises to remove your pain forever in heaven.

TODAY'S PLAN

Where do you hurt the most—in your body or your heart? Can you try to find God in your pain instead of trying to completely remove it?

OPPRESSION

TODAY'S PROMISE

Be strong in the Lord and in his mighty power. Put on all of God's armor so that you will be able to stand firm against all strategies of the devil. For we are not fighting against flesh-and-blood enemies, but against evil rulers and authorities of the unseen world, against mighty powers in this dark world, and against evil spirits in the heavenly places.　—EPHESIANS 6:10–12

TODAY'S THOUGHT

When Satan has you under his control, you are spiritually oppressed. It wears you down until you fall into sin, and then it keeps you from seeking God's help. But God is a warrior. He is always ready to fight on your behalf, always ready to come to your defense. Join with God in the battle, or you will be vulnerable and helpless in the face of the enemy's attacks. God promises that with him you are guaranteed victory.

TODAY'S PLAN

Are you armed for the battle against Satan?

FAITH

TODAY'S PROMISE

Abram believed the LORD, and the LORD counted him as righteous because of his faith.

—GENESIS 15:6

Anyone who believes in me will live, even after dying.

—JOHN 11:25

TODAY'S THOUGHT

Abram made many mistakes, so how could God call him righteous? Despite his bad choices, Abram believed and trusted in God. It was faith, not perfection, that made him right in God's eyes. This same principle is true for you. Rather than measuring your goodness, God is looking at your faith and your willingness to follow him. When the Lord sees your faith, he declares you righteous.

TODAY'S PLAN

Are you more interested in having faith or trying to be good?

HEAVEN

TODAY'S PROMISE

This world is not our permanent home; we are looking forward to a home yet to come.

—HEBREWS 13:14

TODAY'S THOUGHT

Here on earth, you will live for a hundred years or less. In heaven, a hundred *million* years is just the beginning! Yet God has determined that how you live during your short time on earth will prepare you for heaven. This gives you purpose in your life, perspective on your troubles, and anticipation for what God has planned for you in eternity.

TODAY'S PLAN

How is your life here on earth preparing you for life in heaven? How can you live now to prepare for eternity?

EMOTIONS

TODAY'S PROMISE

The Holy Spirit produces this kind of fruit in our lives: love, joy, peace, patience, kindness, goodness, faithfulness, gentleness, and self-control.

—GALATIANS 5:22-23

TODAY'S THOUGHT

We often think of emotions negatively because they tend to get out of control. But without emotions, you could not experience the power and satisfaction of a relationship with God, nor could you model the character of God in your life. Don't deny your emotions, but don't let them control you or cause you to sin. Allow the emotions God has given you to deepen your relationship with him. They will help you experience the drama and power of the Christian life and have a profound impact on the people around you.

TODAY'S PLAN

Which emotions help you feel closer to God?

JUSTICE

TODAY'S PROMISE

This is what the LORD says: "Be just and fair to all. Do what is right and good, for I am coming soon to rescue you and to display my righteousness among you. Blessed are all those who are careful to do this." —ISAIAH 56:1-2

TODAY'S THOUGHT

When you are experiencing difficult times, it is tempting to think God is not fair or just. How can he allow a Christian to suffer when so many unbelievers are prospering? The Bible tells us that in this life justice and fairness will often be perverted by selfish people. But God promises that justice will not be twisted forever. True justice will one day prevail in eternity for those who live for God. So keep fighting for justice now, and rest in the fact that God will set everything right in the future.

TODAY'S PLAN

How can you focus less on your own injustices and more on bringing justice to those who are oppressed?

SEEKING GOD

TODAY'S PROMISE

*God has made everything beautiful for its own time.
He has planted eternity in the human heart, but
even so, people cannot see the whole scope of God's
work from beginning to end.* —ECCLESIASTES 3:11

If you seek him, you will find him.

—1 CHRONICLES 28:9

TODAY'S THOUGHT

In your heart you know there is someone or
something out there that is much bigger than
yourself. It is your conscience that tells you this;
God has given every human being this innate
sense of his existence. If you listen to your conscience, you will begin a search that God
promises will lead you to him.

TODAY'S PLAN

*Are you on a quest for God? He promises that those who
seek him will find him.*

CONTENTMENT

TODAY'S PROMISE

The LORD is my shepherd; I have all that I need.

—PSALM 23:1

O God, . . . give me neither poverty nor riches! Give me just enough to satisfy my needs. For if I grow rich, I may deny you and say, "Who is the LORD?"

—PROVERBS 30:7-9

TODAY'S THOUGHT

Contentment means enjoying the blessings God has given you, which should lead you to remember him and thank him rather than forgetting or ignoring him. It is dangerous to find contentment in things that ultimately fail the test of eternity—possessions, money, food, accomplishments, social status. When these things fail, your contentment will also fade away. True contentment comes only through your relationship with God, who never fails.

TODAY'S PLAN

Where do you find contentment?

MEDITATION

TODAY'S PROMISE

You will keep in perfect peace all who trust in you, all whose thoughts are fixed on you! —ISAIAH 26:3

TODAY'S THOUGHT

Meditation is setting aside time to intentionally think about God, talk to him, listen to him, read his Word, and study the writings of other Christians. If you don't spend any time connecting with God, how can you expect to know what he wants from you? Meditation connects you with God, restoring your confidence in his promises, your passion for what he has called you to do, and your commitment to follow him. When you meditate on God's Word, you remember who he is and what he has done, giving you the assurance that he has much yet in store for you.

TODAY'S PLAN

How can you find more time to intentionally connect with God?

WORDS

TODAY'S PROMISE

If you claim to be religious but don't control your tongue, you are fooling yourself, and your religion is worthless.

—JAMES 1:26

TODAY'S THOUGHT

Exercising self-control over your words includes knowing what you should say and what you shouldn't say. How often do you even take notice of what comes out of your mouth? Ask a friend to help you make a list of the positive and negative words you typically speak. To stop the negative words, ask yourself before you say something, "Is it true? Is it kind? Is it helpful?" If you can answer yes to these questions, your positive words will have an amazing impact on others.

TODAY'S PLAN

How can you make sure you have more positive than negative words coming from your mouth and heart?

FORGETTING

TODAY'S PROMISE

The same happens to all who forget God. The hopes of the godless evaporate. Their confidence hangs by a thread. They are leaning on a spider's web.

—JOB 8:13-14

TODAY'S THOUGHT

When you forget God, you have nothing left but sin and yourself, which leaves you no hope for your eternal future. Forgetting God will turn you over to the consequences of sin without the benefits of God's gracious mercy. So that you don't forget God, remember how you have seen his hand at work in your past, tell others what he is doing in your life now, and meditate on his Word to see how he promises to work in your future.

TODAY'S PLAN

Are you in danger of forgetting about God?

JUNE 26

PRESENCE OF GOD

TODAY'S PROMISE

You go before me and follow me. You place your hand of blessing on my head. . . . I can never escape from your Spirit! I can never get away from your presence!
—PSALM 139:5-7

TODAY'S THOUGHT

God's Word, the Bible, promises that when you have a relationship with God, his presence is always with you. When you believe this promise, you will begin to see the events in your life as evidence of God's presence with you and love for you rather than random chance.

TODAY'S PLAN

How well do you see the evidence of God's presence in your life?

COVETING

TODAY'S PROMISE

Wherever there is jealousy and selfish ambition, there you will find disorder and evil of every kind.

—JAMES 3:16

TODAY'S THOUGHT

Coveting is selfishly desiring what you cannot or should not have. It can cause you to stop thinking rationally and start to scheme. If coveting is left unchecked, you can become obsessed with getting what you want, even if it means taking it from someone else. The consequences could take many forms, but they will certainly damage your relationship with others and with God. Jealousy makes you more self-centered instead of others-centered, and the Christian life is all about being others-centered.

TODAY'S PLAN

Is there anything you're coveting right now?

STEWARDSHIP

TODAY'S PROMISE

The earth is the LORD's, and everything in it. The world and all its people belong to him. —PSALM 24:1

Yes, each of us will give a personal account to God. —ROMANS 14:12

TODAY'S THOUGHT

If a friend loaned you his new car, you'd make every effort to care for it and use it well. Everything you have is on loan to you from God. He owns it all, and he lets you use it. Make sure you are a good steward of everything he has entrusted to your care because someday you will have to give an account for how you handled what he gave you.

TODAY'S PLAN

What is your attitude toward the things God has entrusted to your care? How can you be a better steward of earth's resources? of your relationships? of your possessions?

HONESTY

TODAY'S PROMISE

Yes, what joy for those whose record the LORD has cleared of sin, whose lives are lived in complete honesty!

—PSALM 32:2

TODAY'S THOUGHT

Honest choices allow you to live at peace with yourself, to be free from sin and holy in God's sight, and to gain the trust of others. Dishonest choices only weave a web of deception, causing you to tell more and more lies to cover your tracks. A habit of dishonesty will eventually lead to humiliation.

TODAY'S PLAN

Can you commit today to not telling a single lie and not giving yourself credit for something you didn't do?

FAILURE

TODAY'S PROMISE

Each time [the Lord] said, "My grace is all you need. My power works best in weakness." So now I am glad to boast about my weaknesses, so that the power of Christ can work through me. That's why I take pleasure in my weaknesses, and in the insults, hardships, persecutions, and troubles that I suffer for Christ. For when I am weak, then I am strong. —2 CORINTHIANS 12:9-10

TODAY'S THOUGHT

One thing is certain: You must learn to live with failure. In fact, you must embrace it because it is in your failures that God's power works best in you. Everyone has weaknesses. Everyone fails— a lot. The key to success is not the number of times you fail but the way you respond to failure. Those who admit their failures can look forward to an extra measure of God's strength to help them through their failures and on to greater things.

TODAY'S PLAN

The next time you fail, look forward to God releasing more of his power in your life.

JULY

LAZINESS

Work hard and become a leader; be lazy and become a slave.
—PROVERBS 12:24

We often think of sin as doing something we should not do, but sin can also be failing to do something we should. If you are not dealing with some of your responsibilities or not confronting someone because you are afraid of the consequences, you might be falling into the sin of laziness. Lazy people are self-centered and do not want to take the time to do what they should. A spiritually lazy person may fail to notice temptation until it is too late. You must confront yourself or the enemy, and you must have the discipline to avoid whatever distracts you from what God wants you to do.

What causes you to neglect doing what you should?

PROTECTION

TODAY'S PROMISE

Those who live in the shelter of the Most High will find rest in the shadow of the Almighty. . . . His faithful promises are your armor and protection. Do not be afraid of the terrors of the night, nor the arrow that flies in the day. . . . Though a thousand fall at your side, though ten thousand are dying around you, these evils will not touch you. . . . For he will order his angels to protect you wherever you go.

—PSALM 91:4-5, 11

TODAY'S THOUGHT

This passage of Scripture has been a constant source of courage and encouragement throughout the centuries. It reminds you that while the threats of this world are seemingly endless, the promise of God's eternal protection is infinitely greater. The physical death we must face on this earth is simply the door to eternal life with God.

TODAY'S PLAN

How does knowing the extent of God's protection help you live more courageously?

HOLINESS

Work at living in peace with everyone, and work at living a holy life, for those who are not holy will not see the Lord. —HEBREWS 12:14

TODAY'S THOUGHT

Holiness is an indicator of the health of your relationship with God. Being holy includes trying your best to treat others with the same mercy and unconditional love that God would show them—and that God has shown you. You won't achieve perfect holiness in this life, but God asks that you sincerely try to be more like him each day. The more you understand what the Holy One has done for you, the more you will want to live the holy life he desires.

TODAY'S PLAN

How can you live out God's peace and holiness in your relationships with others?

DEPENDENCE

TODAY'S PROMISE

God . . . will supply all your needs from his glorious riches, which have been given to us in Christ Jesus.

—PHILIPPIANS 4:19

TODAY'S THOUGHT

God loves to help those who depend on him. He helps you by providing resources to meet your needs. God has a full supply house and a ready supply system that are free for the asking, but you must ask.

TODAY'S PLAN

What kind of help could you use from God? Are you depending on him to supply it?

REVENGE

TODAY'S PROMISE

Never pay back evil with more evil. . . . Never take revenge. Leave that to the righteous anger of God. For the Scriptures say, "I will take revenge; I will pay them back," says the LORD. —ROMANS 12:17-19

TODAY'S THOUGHT

Seeking revenge is a basic instinct of our sinful human nature. Whether we are cut off in traffic, unjustly criticized, or the victim of a violent crime, our gut response is to get revenge. But the Bible tells us that one wrongdoing never justifies another. Getting back at someone only sends you into a downward spiral of sin and retaliation. Instead, you should refuse to take revenge on those who mistreat you. God promises that he will bring good out of a bad situation.

TODAY'S PLAN

If someone has wronged you, how can you turn your desire for revenge over to God?

STRENGTH

TODAY'S PROMISE

You formed the mountains by your power and armed yourself with mighty strength. —PSALM 65:6

Look up into the heavens. Who created all the stars? He brings them out like an army, one after another, calling each by its name. Because of his great power and incomparable strength, not a single one is missing. —ISAIAH 40:26

TODAY'S THOUGHT

God's mighty power is evident all around us in his creation. God created and sustains the universe. He has named every star. The great message of the Bible is that this awesome and almighty God, who parted the waters of the sea and puts the stars in the sky, offers you his strength each day. Will you accept it?

TODAY'S PLAN

The next time you wonder how powerful God really is, look for the evidence of his strength in the natural world around you. What does it reveal about God?

CONFIDENCE

TODAY'S PROMISE

God can be trusted to keep his promise.

—HEBREWS 10:23

TODAY'S THOUGHT

How much you trust others depends on how confident you are that they can be trusted. You can be completely confident in what God's Word says because God has never broken a single promise. He will always do what he says.

TODAY'S PLAN

How confident are you that God will fulfill his promises? What can you do to increase your confidence?

FRIENDSHIP

TODAY'S PROMISE

My heart has heard you say, "Come and talk with me." And my heart responds, "LORD, I am coming."
—PSALM 27:8

Come close to God, and God will come close to you.
—JAMES 4:8

TODAY'S THOUGHT

You do your best to stay in touch with your close friends, and it should be no different with God. He promises that as you draw close to him, he will draw close to you. Read his Word daily, and listen to what he says in it. Pray constantly. Remember that God is with you all the time and you can talk to him about anything. Share your thoughts, needs, and concerns with him. As you practice coming into God's presence, you'll begin to build the friendship you desire.

TODAY'S PLAN

Think of the ways you maintain and strengthen your friendships. How can you apply those principles to your relationship with God?

SERVING

TODAY'S PROMISE

Among you it will be different. Whoever wants to be a leader among you must be your servant, and whoever wants to be first among you must be the slave of everyone else.

—MARK 10:43-44

TODAY'S THOUGHT

A popular conception of wealth and success is being able to afford the luxury of having servants. Jesus turns this thinking on its head by teaching that the highest goal in life is to be a servant. He places such a high value on serving because it is centered on others rather than yourself, and serving others is the essence of effective Christian living. God promises that those who serve others will be the most highly regarded in his Kingdom.

TODAY'S PLAN

How can you serve God today by humbly serving someone else?

COMFORT

TODAY'S PROMISE

Jesus said, "Come to me, all of you who are weary and carry heavy burdens, and I will give you rest."

—MATTHEW 11:28

TODAY'S THOUGHT

When tragedy strikes or problems overwhelm you, do you wonder what happened to God? Do you wonder why he would allow these things to happen? Nagging doubts might cause you to question whether God still loves you. When you lose confidence that God cares about you, you are in danger of pushing him away and separating yourself from your only source of hope. When tough times come, move immediately toward God, not away from him. You will receive comfort and gain perspective.

TODAY'S PLAN

Do you still believe that God cares about you even when trouble comes your way? How can you learn to expect his comfort instead of doubting his presence?

THOUGHTS

Don't copy the behavior and customs of this world, but let God transform you into a new person by changing the way you think. Then you will learn to know God's will for you, which is good and pleasing and perfect.   —ROMANS 12:2

TODAY'S THOUGHT

God is pleased when you think about him. What you think about reveals who you really are on the inside. In other words, the quality of your thoughts is an important measure of the condition of your heart. For example, if you are consistently thanking God for what you have, those thoughts of gratitude come from a grateful heart. If you are constantly complaining about your circumstances, those negative thoughts come from an ungrateful heart. When God transforms your heart, thoughts of thankfulness, praise, love, and joy will soon follow.

TODAY'S PLAN

What do you think about the most? Do you need to change your thought life?

SIN

TODAY'S PROMISE

The path of the virtuous leads away from evil;
whoever follows that path is safe. —PROVERBS 16:17

TODAY'S THOUGHT

Having a close relationship with God will help
you avoid sin. The closer you are to him, the
further you are from evil and the less likely you
are to sin. Seek direction from the Lord, and
you will avoid many mistakes in judgment.

TODAY'S PLAN

Is there a particular sin you need to work hard to avoid?

GENEROSITY

TODAY'S PROMISE

Remember this—a farmer who plants only a few seeds will get a small crop. But the one who plants generously will get a generous crop.

—2 CORINTHIANS 9:6

TODAY'S THOUGHT

You should not give in order to grow richer, but your resources will grow when you give more. What you receive in return may be spiritual or relational rather than material. One of the great paradoxes of the Christian life is that the more generously you give, the more God blesses you in some way. One of the reasons for this is that the same qualities that make you responsible and trustworthy also make you generous. But the primary reason is that God in his grace entrusts more to you so that you can be a greater channel for bringing his blessings into this world.

TODAY'S PLAN

How generous are you with the resources God has given you?

SUPERNATURAL

TODAY'S PROMISE

We have received God's Spirit (not the world's spirit), so we can know the wonderful things God has freely given us. —1 CORINTHIANS 2:12

TODAY'S THOUGHT

God's presence within you in the form of the Holy Spirit is evidence of the supernatural. The Holy Spirit teaches and instructs your heart in the ways of God, revealing things to you that you cannot see with your eyes. The Holy Spirit helps you recognize how God works and empowers you in life-changing ways: to love others even when they hurt you, to find peace in the midst of suffering, to think of others before yourself. The Holy Spirit gives you the assurance that there is a God, that he is at work in the world, and that you belong to him.

TODAY'S PLAN

How does the Holy Spirit assure you of God's presence in your life?

ATTITUDE

TODAY'S PROMISE

Anyone with ears to hear should listen and understand. . . . To those who listen to my teaching, more understanding will be given, and they will have an abundance of knowledge. But for those who are not listening, even what little understanding they have will be taken away from them.

—MATTHEW 13:9, 12

TODAY'S THOUGHT

Listening is not merely an action, it's also an attitude. Are you interested in and open to what others have to say? Are you open to what God, the creator of wisdom, has to say? If your attitude is one of respect and openness to God's advice, you will learn truths that will change your life forever. A willing attitude and an open heart bring the rewards of wisdom, understanding, knowledge, and success.

TODAY'S PLAN

How much do you pay attention to God during the course of your day? Do you need to change your attitude to notice him more?

CONSEQUENCES

TODAY'S PROMISE

You will always harvest what you plant.

—GALATIANS 6:7

TODAY'S THOUGHT

A consequence is an outcome, aftermath, or result. Some actions produce consequences that are neither morally good nor bad. For example, if you take a shower, you will get clean. But many thoughts and actions have definite good or bad consequences. Sin will always cause bad consequences. Faithfulness to God will always result in good consequences. Before you act, ask yourself, *What will the consequences of my actions be?*

TODAY'S PLAN

Have you thought through the consequences of what you plan to do and say today?

JULY 17

DISCERNMENT

TODAY'S PROMISE

My child, don't lose sight of common sense and discernment. Hang on to them, for they will refresh your soul. They are like jewels on a necklace. They keep you safe on your way, and your feet will not stumble. —PROVERBS 3:21-23

TODAY'S THOUGHT

Discernment is the ability to differentiate between right and wrong, true and false, good and bad, important and trivial, godly and ungodly. Discernment helps you properly interpret issues and understand the motives of people who might have a certain agenda. Discernment shows you the way through the maze of options you face. When you practice discernment and train yourself to detect right from wrong, you can avoid the pitfalls and confusion so many people fall into. God promises that discernment will keep you safe in the way that he wants you to go.

TODAY'S PLAN

How can you practice better discernment?

CHURCH

TODAY'S PROMISE

Just as our bodies have many parts and each part has a special function, so it is with Christ's body. We are many parts of one body, and we all belong to each other. —ROMANS 12:4-5

TODAY'S THOUGHT

God has given every believer special gifts. Some are great organizers and leaders, while others are gifted musicians, helpers, even dishwashers! When those in the body of Christ use their gifts to serve each other, the church becomes a powerful force for good, a strong witness for Jesus, and a mighty army to combat Satan's attacks against the people in their community. The church needs you! The body of Christ is not complete unless you are functioning within it.

TODAY'S PLAN

What special function do you have within the church?

DISAPPOINTMENT

TODAY'S PROMISE

They cried out to you and were saved. They trusted in you and were never disgraced.   —PSALM 22:5

TODAY'S THOUGHT

Disappointment in some form may haunt you almost every day. If you let disappointment dominate your thoughts, you will become negative, sad, and depressed. Life is full of disappointment; you often disappoint God with your sins. God doesn't want you to dwell on what could have been but on what can be. He is the God of hope. That's why he sent his Son, Jesus, so you could stand before him as more than good enough. You are holy in his eyes! The next time you feel disappointed, remember everything you have, use the time to grow, and be happy that you have the approval of the One who really matters.

TODAY'S PLAN

With the knowledge that God loves you and turns bad into good, what can you learn from a recent disappointment in your life?

SAFETY

TODAY'S PROMISE

You are my hiding place; you protect me from trouble. You surround me with songs of victory.

—PSALM 32:7

TODAY'S THOUGHT

Peace comes from knowing that God is always watching over you, day and night. This doesn't mean that your body will never be harmed, but it does mean that God will never let Satan snatch you away from him. You can have absolute confidence that you will be safely his forever.

TODAY'S PLAN

Do you feel safe in God's arms? How should this change the way you look at the future?

CHARACTER

TODAY'S PROMISE

"Let's feast and drink, for tomorrow we die!" Don't be fooled by those who say such things, for "bad company corrupts good character."

—1 CORINTHIANS 15:32-33

TODAY'S THOUGHT

If you didn't believe in resurrection and eternal life, then it might make sense to live a lifestyle that seeks only after pleasure. As a student, your character is often tested through peer pressure from those who live only for the moment, indulging in sinful behaviors such as drunkenness, sexual sin, defying authority, or gossiping. You don't have to completely avoid being in the company of such people because you can be a godly influence in their lives. But if you spend too much time with them and don't make your convictions clear, the Bible says you will become more like them instead of the other way around. Without godly friends to hold you accountable, you are not as strong as you think.

TODAY'S PLAN

Do you have friends who share your values and encourage you in godly living?

MIRACLES

"Yes," says the LORD, "I will do mighty miracles for you, like those I did when I rescued you from slavery in Egypt."
—MICAH 7:15

Maybe you think a miracle is always a dramatic event, like the dead being raised back to life. But miracles are happening all around you. These supernatural occurrences may not be as dramatic as the parting of the Red Sea, but they are no less powerful. Think of the birth of a baby, the healing of an illness, the rebirth of the earth in spring, the restoration of broken relationships through the work of love and forgiveness, the salvation of sinners through faith alone, the specific call of God in your life. And these are just a few "everyday" miracles. If you think you've never seen a miracle, look closer—they are happening all around you!

How can you be more open to seeing the miracles in your life?

FEAR OF GOD

TODAY'S PROMISE

Fear of the LORD is the foundation of wisdom. Knowledge of the Holy One results in good judgment.

—PROVERBS 9:10

TODAY'S THOUGHT

To fear the Lord is to recognize that he is holy, almighty, righteous, all-knowing, and wise. When you have the proper understanding of God, you also gain a clearer picture of yourself as sinful, weak, and needy. The only fitting response to the God of the universe, who loves you despite your failures, is to fall at his feet in humble awe. When you fear the Lord by displaying this attitude of humility and reverence, he promises to give you wisdom and joy.

TODAY'S PLAN

What might you gain from developing a proper fear of God?

MONEY

TODAY'S PROMISE

Honor the LORD with your wealth and with the best part of everything you produce. —PROVERBS 3:9

The trustworthy person will get a rich reward, but a person who wants quick riches will get into trouble. —PROVERBS 28:20

TODAY'S THOUGHT

Money can be a valuable tool for helping to accomplish God's work here on earth, so money itself is not evil—but the love of money can be. Money is dangerous when it deceives you into thinking that wealth will solve all of your problems. Loving money is sinful when you trust it rather than God for your security. Since God gave you the ability to make money, it really belongs to him. The crucial question is not how much of your money you should give to God but how much of God's money you should keep for yourself.

TODAY'S PLAN

Which do you enjoy more—spending your money or sharing it?

CHEATING

TODAY'S PROMISE

If you are faithful in little things, you will be faithful in large ones. But if you are dishonest in little things, you won't be honest with greater responsibilities. And if you are untrustworthy about worldly wealth, who will trust you with the true riches of heaven?
—LUKE 16:10-11

TODAY'S THOUGHT

Your character is tested in the small choices you make. Cheating in a little thing is cut out of the same piece of cloth as cheating in a big way. Just as a small drop of dye will color even a large glass of clear water, a small act of deception colors your whole character. God promises that when you are honest and faithful in small ways, he will give you more and greater opportunities to do good.

TODAY'S PLAN

Are you honest in even the smallest things?

FRUSTRATION

TODAY'S PROMISE

Even when you do ask, you don't get it because your whole motive is wrong—you want only what will give you pleasure.

—JAMES 4:3

TODAY'S THOUGHT

At times you may feel frustrated in your prayers. You keep expecting answers that don't seem to come. But you may be failing to see the bigger picture of the way God is answering you. God loves to give good things to his children, but he often withholds things that would only fulfill selfish desires. There's a big difference between being frustrated in your quest to do good and being frustrated because you are not getting your own way.

TODAY'S PLAN

Have you felt frustrated in your prayers? Is it because you're not getting your own way? Try asking God for what he wants rather than what you want.

CONSISTENCY

We can be sure that we know him if we obey his commandments.
—1 JOHN 2:3

The key to living a perfect life is obeying all of God's commandments. But no one is perfect. That's why Jesus Christ died on the cross and rose again—to forgive your sins. The key, then, is to consistently try to obey God's commandments, realizing that you will fail sometimes. Then at the point of your failure, consistently seek Jesus and his forgiveness. Consistency in these things is evidence that you belong to him.

Are you consistently trying to obey God's commandments?

DOUBT

TODAY'S PROMISE

Patient endurance is what you need now, so you will continue to do God's will. Then you will receive all that he has promised. —HEBREWS 10:36

TODAY'S THOUGHT

When you begin to doubt and wonder if what you believe is really true, you simply need to be obedient during this time of testing. Doubt can be spiritually healthy or unhealthy, depending on what you do with it. You can allow doubt to destroy your faith, or you can let it lead you back to God. Bring your questions to God, and he will turn them into faith.

TODAY'S PLAN

Do you ever bring your questions directly to God during times of doubt? What questions would you like to ask him today?

SEDUCTION

TODAY'S PROMISE

If righteous people turn away from their righteous behavior and ignore the obstacles I put in their way, they will die. —EZEKIEL 3:20

Guard your heart above all else, for it determines the course of your life. —PROVERBS 4:23

TODAY'S THOUGHT

Most often we think of seduction within the context of a sexual encounter, but it is actually a tactic that Satan often uses to disguise sin with beauty, power, riches, pleasure, even good deeds. Seduction tempts us to accept an immediate high at the risk of hurtful and even devastating long-term consequences. Seduction takes something that is good out of context and turns it into sin. When you give your whole self—both body and soul—to God, you will have the power to do what is right instead of giving in to seduction.

TODAY'S PLAN

Is Satan trying to seduce you right now?

WORK

TODAY'S PROMISE

To enjoy your work and accept your lot in life—this is indeed a gift from God. —ECCLESIASTES 5:19

TODAY'S THOUGHT

Whether your work is being a full-time student or you work a part-time job in addition to your studies, you can be sure that work is part of God's plan for your life and that your work matters to God. Those who work diligently experience many blessings and are able to pass them on to others. At its best, work honors God and brings meaning and joy to life. In your work, you should model characteristics of God's work, such as excellence, concern for the well-being of others, purpose, creativity, and service. When you have the perspective that you are actually working for God, your focus moves off the task itself and allows you to enjoy your work.

TODAY'S PLAN

How can you honor God through the work you will do today?

DIRECTION

TODAY'S PROMISE

I know the LORD is always with me. I will not be shaken, for he is right beside me. . . . You will show me the way of life, granting me the joy of your presence and the pleasures of living with you forever.

—PSALM 16:8, 11

TODAY'S THOUGHT

Those who follow God will often take a very different path through life than those who follow someone or something else. God promises great rewards to those who follow him, not the least of which is eternal life with him. If you want to follow God's direction for your life, you must go where he leads. And the only way to follow God is to stay close enough so you can keep your eyes on him. Then God promises to show you which direction he wants you to go.

TODAY'S PLAN

In what direction are you headed?

AUGUST

VULNERABILITY

TODAY'S PROMISE

There is no condemnation for those who belong to Christ Jesus. And because you belong to him, the power of the life-giving Spirit has freed you from the power of sin that leads to death. —ROMANS 8:1-2

TODAY'S THOUGHT

We often resist being vulnerable with God because of our sins, especially the ones we don't really want to give up. But vulnerability requires full disclosure, not hiding or covering up. It is only through vulnerability that you will find true healing, restoration, renewal, and forgiveness. When you are vulnerable with God about the sin in your life, it allows his forgiveness to free you from your old way of life and his divine healing to bring you into a life of godliness. You will have the desire and the confidence to be increasingly vulnerable with God and others.

TODAY'S PLAN

Do others know who you really are, deep down inside? How can you be more vulnerable with God?

PEER PRESSURE

TODAY'S PROMISE

As pressure and stress bear down on me, I find joy in your commands. —PSALM 119:143

TODAY'S THOUGHT

Some of the pressure you face comes from friends who try to persuade you to do things you don't want to do. Before you do what others want, first think about what God wants. When you take time to consider his advice, as found in the Bible, you will know if your peers are trying to persuade you to do the wrong thing. It's easier to resist bad influences when you are grounded in God's Word and committed to obeying it. You will have joy when you know you are pleasing God and doing what is right.

TODAY'S PLAN

Do you know the Bible well enough to know when someone is asking you to contradict it?

SECURITY

TODAY'S PROMISE

Those who trust in the LORD are as secure as Mount Zion; they will not be defeated but will endure forever.
—PSALM 125:1

I cling to you; your strong right hand holds me securely.
—PSALM 63:8

TODAY'S THOUGHT

Trust is the basis for security; it means having confidence that you can count on certain things to be true. And who can be trusted more than God? When you believe his promises, you will begin to feel more secure. You will trust that you can always count on what he says. And what could be more reassuring than God's promise of eternal security?

TODAY'S PLAN

What can you do today to increase your feelings of security?

CREATIVITY

We are God's masterpiece. He has created us anew in Christ Jesus, so we can do the good things he planned for us long ago. —EPHESIANS 2:10

TODAY'S THOUGHT

God created you to do good things, and to do good things you must be creative. He created you with creativity for the specific purpose of carrying out the work he created you to do. God gives you the gift of creativity so that you can express yourself in potentially millions of different ways—through worship, singing, loving, helping, playing music, crafting things, thinking through problems. When your creativity accomplishes the work God wants you to do, you become a masterpiece, a beautiful expression of God's image doing God's work for God's people.

TODAY'S PLAN

How are you using your creativity to accomplish what God created you to do?

CONSCIENCE

TODAY'S PROMISE

Cling to your faith in Christ, and keep your conscience clear. For some people have deliberately violated their consciences; as a result, their faith has been shipwrecked.

—1 TIMOTHY 1:19

TODAY'S THOUGHT

God's Word says that if you ignore your conscience, your faith will be shipwrecked. When you sin, you are deliberately going against your conscience. You know what you are doing is wrong because your conscience tells you it is, but you do it anyway because sin is often so appealing. If you continually do what your conscience tells you not to, eventually you will no longer hear it warning you of danger. Without a strong conscience, you become desensitized to sin and your heart becomes hardened. The key to a healthy conscience is faith in Jesus Christ.

TODAY'S PLAN

Have you been listening to your conscience or ignoring it? Your answer will tell you if you are growing in your faith or neglecting it.

DEATH

TODAY'S PROMISE

Don't be afraid of those who want to kill your body; they cannot touch your soul. —MATTHEW 10:28

TODAY'S THOUGHT

Why are we so afraid to die? Often it is because we are uncertain about what happens after death. Even though life is hard at times, this life is all we know; death represents the unknown. But fear of dying could indicate a weak relationship with God or a misunderstanding of heaven. The more real God is to you, the more certain you will become about what happens after death, so the less fearsome death will be. Because we are afraid to die, we often pray that God will protect us. God often does protect you from physical harm, but he is more concerned about protecting your soul from eternal harm. When you commit your life to following his ways, he commits to bringing you safely into eternity with him.

TODAY'S PLAN

Are you afraid of death?

CONTENTMENT

TODAY'S PROMISE

I have learned how to be content with whatever I have. I know how to live on almost nothing or with everything. I have learned the secret of living in every situation. —PHILIPPIANS 4:11-12

TODAY'S THOUGHT

If you always want more, you will always be dissatisfied with what you have. It's human nature to think you would be happier if you had just a little more. The secret of happiness, however, is learning to be content with what you already have, whether it is much or little, and learning to make the most of whatever God has given you. Then you enjoy whatever God puts in front of you each day rather than looking past it to something you may never have.

TODAY'S PLAN

What things do you already have that you can be content with?

MOTIVES

TODAY'S PROMISE

*The LORD's light penetrates the human spirit,
exposing every hidden motive.* —PROVERBS 20:27

TODAY'S THOUGHT

One person may give money to the church in
order to earn a tax break; another person may
do it to send missionaries to a place where no
one knows about Jesus. The same act of giving
can be set in motion by very different motives.
The Bible teaches that God is as interested in
our motives as he is in our behavior. Selfish
and sinful motives eventually produce selfish
and sinful behavior, but good and godly motives
result in true good works.

TODAY'S PLAN

*Evaluate every decision you make today. How many
of your actions are based on good motives rather than
selfish ones?*

BOREDOM

TODAY'S PROMISE

Our great desire is that you will keep right on loving others as long as life lasts, in order to make certain that what you hope for will come true. Then you will not become spiritually dull and indifferent.

—HEBREWS 6:11-12

TODAY'S THOUGHT

Being a Christian might seem boring to many people—"Don't do this," "You can't do that." But those who understand what the Christian life is all about find it full and exciting. When you realize that almighty God wants to work through you to accomplish his work in the world, you will be amazed to see the wonderful opportunities he puts before you. Focus on using and developing your God-given gifts, and look forward to the eternal rewards God promises to believers—then your life will always be exciting! If you become bored in your Christian life, try making yourself available to God and asking him to pour out his blessings through you to others.

TODAY'S PLAN

Are you bored with life? Ask God to open your eyes to the spiritual adventure he has in store for you.

BLESSING

TODAY'S PROMISE

Don't repay evil for evil. Don't retaliate with insults when people insult you. Instead, pay them back with a blessing. That is what God has called you to do, and he will bless you for it. —1 PETER 3:9

TODAY'S THOUGHT

When people hurt us, our immediate instinct is to retaliate: *I'll show them! They need to learn a lesson.* But the Bible says we must have the opposite response. Instead of retaliating when others hurt us, we are to bless them! We are to pray for them, asking God to change their hearts. God promises that he will bless you for doing this. And enjoying God's blessings is far better than feeling angry or retaliating.

TODAY'S PLAN

The next time someone hurts you, can you be prepared to bless instead of retaliate?

CONTROL

TODAY'S PROMISE

He existed before anything else, and he holds all creation together.   —COLOSSIANS 1:17

TODAY'S THOUGHT

A God who is powerful enough to create the
earth, the planets, and all the heavens is certainly
the supreme ruler of all things. He is even Lord
of all the unseen spiritual forces, and he can be
trusted with ultimate control of the universe.
If God gave up his control over the earth, if the
forces of nature—gravity, for example—ceased
to function, the world would end in a moment.
You are part of God's creation, which he holds
together, so you can certainly trust him to have
control over the outcome of your life.

TODAY'S PLAN

*Do you trust that God is holding everything together even
when you feel like life is falling apart?*

POTENTIAL

TODAY'S PROMISE

I press on to possess that perfection for which Christ Jesus first possessed me. No, dear brothers and sisters, I have not achieved it, but . . . forgetting the past and looking forward to what lies ahead, I press on to reach the end of the race and receive the heavenly prize for which God, through Christ Jesus, is calling us. —PHILIPPIANS 3:12-14

TODAY'S THOUGHT

The bad news is that you will never realize your full potential in this life because your human nature is sinful and therefore you can't be perfect. But you can achieve much of your potential when God works through you. Reaching your God-given potential will not happen overnight, but with small, steady steps each day, you'll be headed in the right direction.

TODAY'S PLAN

Can you even begin to imagine the potential that God sees in you?

FULFILLMENT

TODAY'S PROMISE

Jesus replied, "I am the bread of life. Whoever comes to me will never be hungry again. Whoever believes in me will never be thirsty." —JOHN 6:35

TODAY'S THOUGHT

Every human being has both a body and a soul. It's obvious that we must feed our bodies in order to survive, but so often we neglect to feed our souls. No wonder we feel unfulfilled, like something is missing. Jesus is the nourishment your soul craves. When you feed yourself with his Word, he fills your soul with joy, wisdom, purpose, hope, and truth. Then you will truly be fulfilled.

TODAY'S PLAN

Do you feel unfulfilled? Are you feeding your soul?

CONFUSION

TODAY'S PROMISE

Let us hold tightly without wavering to the hope we affirm, for God can be trusted to keep his promise.

—HEBREWS 10:23

TODAY'S THOUGHT

Confusion often comes when you waver, uncertain of which decision is best. You will always be confused if you don't even know what decisions you should be making, if you don't know what you are looking for. If that's the case for you, there is a way to clear up your confusion. Let God's Word, the Bible, point you in the right direction. Then at least you will know which roads *not* to take, and that will help reduce the confusion in your life. As you continue to read God's Word and hold tightly to it, the bigger decisions in your life will become clearer as well.

TODAY'S PLAN

How can immersing yourself in God's Word decrease the confusion in your life?

POWER OF GOD

TODAY'S PROMISE

We also pray that you will be strengthened with all his glorious power so you will have all the endurance and patience you need. —COLOSSIANS 1:11

TODAY'S THOUGHT

The power of almighty God is available to you, but God doesn't unleash his power in just anyone. You have to get rid of the filthiness of sin by asking God to forgive you and clean you on the inside. You have to be ready and willing. You have to sincerely want his power for the right reasons. As God's power begins to work in you, you will develop endurance and patience to face any problem or crisis that comes your way. Above all, you will have joy in your relationship with God.

TODAY'S PLAN

Have you made yourself available for God's power to work in you?

WORDS

TODAY'S PROMISE

Let everything you say be good and helpful, so that your words will be an encouragement to those who hear them. —EPHESIANS 4:29

TODAY'S THOUGHT

It's really true—what you spend most of your time thinking about is what you end up doing. So when you're tempted to complain, train yourself to pray instead. When you're tempted to gossip, compliment or encourage someone instead. Then your words will be an encouragement to those around you.

TODAY'S PLAN

What are some practical things you can do to improve the quality of the words you speak?

OBEDIENCE

TODAY'S PROMISE

Be strong and very courageous. Be careful to obey all the instructions Moses gave you. Do not deviate from them, turning either to the right or to the left. Then you will be successful in everything you do. . . . Be strong and courageous! Do not be afraid or discouraged. For the LORD your God is with you wherever you go. —JOSHUA 1:7-9

TODAY'S THOUGHT

To maintain balance between waiting patiently on God and stepping out in faith, you need to courageously obey God's call, one day at a time. You may think you can't accomplish the great work God has planned for you, but you can do smaller tasks for God today while you wait for him to show you the way. When you take small steps of obedience each day, you may eventually find that you have built a great work for him one stone at a time.

TODAY'S PLAN

What small step of faith and obedience can you take today?

EVIL

TODAY'S PROMISE

Why do the wicked get away with despising God? They think, "God will never call us to account." . . . The LORD is king forever and ever! The godless nations will vanish from the land.

—PSALM 10:13, 16

TODAY'S THOUGHT

Sometimes it seems as if evil people can do anything they want—and not only do they get away with it, they flourish. God has promised, however, that in his time, everyone will be judged, evil will be exposed, and the righteous will prevail. God doesn't promise the absence of evil on this earth. In fact, he warns that evil will be pervasive and powerful. But God does promise to help you stand against evil.

TODAY'S PLAN

Stop asking why some people get away with evil and start asking God to give you the strength to combat evil when you come face-to-face with it.

BURDENS

TODAY'S PROMISE

*Let us strip off every weight that slows us down,
especially the sin that so easily trips us up. And let
us run with endurance the race God has set before us.
We do this by keeping our eyes on Jesus. . . . Think
of all the hostility he endured from sinful people;
then you won't become weary and give up.*

—HEBREWS 12:1-3

TODAY'S THOUGHT

Sin, distractions, pressure, disappointment—
these are like weights tied to our arms and legs,
slowing us down as we try to reach the finish line
of life. You must constantly try to get rid of that
extra weight that burdens you so you can run
toward God with freedom and confidence.
Eventually you will win the race of life and
fall happily into the arms of Jesus at the
finish line.

TODAY'S PLAN

*What burden can you get rid of today so you can run the
race of life more effectively?*

DOUBT

TODAY'S PROMISE

When doubts filled my mind, your comfort gave me renewed hope and cheer.
—PSALM 94:19

TODAY'S THOUGHT

Virtually every biblical hero struggled with doubts about God or about God's ability or desire to help. God doesn't mind when you doubt as long as you continue to seek him in the midst of it. Doubt can become sin if it leads you away from God and into skepticism, cynicism, or hard-heartedness. But God promises that doubt can become a blessing if your honest searching leads you to a better understanding of God and a deeper faith in him. When others see your hope in God even as you struggle with doubt, they will be inspired to follow your example and cling to their faith no matter what their circumstances.

TODAY'S PLAN

When you find yourself doubting God, do you let it move you closer to him or further away?

TRUST

TODAY'S PROMISE

Blessed are those who trust in the LORD and have made the LORD their hope and confidence.

—JEREMIAH 17:7

TODAY'S THOUGHT

God wants you to know him so well that trusting him is a natural part of your relationship with him. As you seek his counsel and commit to obeying his Word, you can trust that he will direct you according to his wisdom and his will.

TODAY'S PLAN

How can you trust God more?

HEALING

TODAY'S PROMISE

A man with leprosy came and knelt in front of Jesus, begging to be healed. "If you are willing, you can heal me and make me clean," he said. Moved with compassion, Jesus reached out and touched him. "I am willing," he said. "Be healed!" Instantly the leprosy disappeared, and the man was healed.
—MARK 1:40-42

TODAY'S THOUGHT

When Jesus touched the leper, he revealed both God's power and compassion for the whole person. God can and does heal people today— through the body's natural processes, medical science, and miraculous means. Jesus may not heal your physical problems in this life, but he promises to heal the disease of sin in anyone who asks.

TODAY'S PLAN

Have you asked Jesus to heal the disease of sin in your life?

DISCERNMENT

TODAY'S PROMISE

People who aren't spiritual can't receive these truths from God's Spirit. It all sounds foolish to them and they can't understand it, for only those who are spiritual can understand what the Spirit means.

—1 CORINTHIANS 2:14

TODAY'S THOUGHT

Spiritual discernment involves learning to listen for the voice of the Holy Spirit, who promises to help you recognize the difference between what is true and what is false. The Holy Spirit speaks to your heart and mind, giving you a God-centered perspective on life. Those who don't have the Holy Spirit aren't spiritual, so they can't possibly have God's understanding. In fact, God's wisdom actually seems foolish to them because God's ways are so different from the world's ways. But if you have God's Spirit in you, you have God's wisdom.

TODAY'S PLAN

Are you allowing God's Holy Spirit to give you spiritual discernment?

LOVE

TODAY'S PROMISE

Three things will last forever—faith, hope, and love—and the greatest of these is love. —1 CORINTHIANS 13:13

TODAY'S THOUGHT

People are more confused than ever about love. Love is the greatest of all human emotions, and it is an attribute of God himself. Love involves unselfish service to others, which is evidence that you truly care even though they may not care in return. Faith is the foundation and content of God's message, and hope is the attitude and focus; but love is the action. Love proves that your faith and hope are genuine.

TODAY'S PLAN

Can you show genuine love to someone today?

FAILURE

TODAY'S PROMISE

The LORD is good and does what is right; he shows the proper path to those who go astray. He leads the humble in doing right, teaching them his way. The LORD leads with unfailing love and faithfulness all who keep his covenant and obey his demands.

—PSALM 25:8-10

TODAY'S THOUGHT

Even if you've made wrong turns in the past, God still wants a relationship with you today. If you humbly admit your sin and are sincere in wanting God's help, he promises to set your feet on the right path again, no matter how often you've failed. Don't label yourself a failure because you've made some wrong turns. God is always ready to help you; he'll never give up on you.

TODAY'S PLAN

Do you think of yourself as a failure? Does it help you to know that God doesn't see you that way?

TRUTH

TODAY'S PROMISE

The word of the LORD holds true, and we can trust everything he does. —PSALM 33:4

TODAY'S THOUGHT

God wants you to be an example of his truthfulness. When you read the Bible every day, God will teach you his truth and train you to live it out. Truth that is lived is even more convincing than truth that is spoken. When you go to the right source to find truth, you will be more confident in living it out.

TODAY'S PLAN

What are some ways you can be a living example of God's truth?

PAIN

TODAY'S PROMISE

In his kindness God called you to share in his eternal glory by means of Christ Jesus. So after you have suffered a little while, he will restore, support, and strengthen you, and he will place you on a firm foundation.

—1 PETER 5:10

TODAY'S THOUGHT

It is easier to deal with pain when someone is helping you through it. Who better to help you than Jesus, who has suffered every kind of hurt and pain this world can dish out? God doesn't necessarily prevent you from experiencing pain, but he will keep you from being defeated by it if you go to him for help and healing. Place your pain on his shoulders so he can help you bear it.

TODAY'S PLAN

When you are hurting, do you go to God for help?

ABILITIES

Thieves are jealous of each other's loot, but the godly are well rooted and bear their own fruit.

—PROVERBS 12:12

TODAY'S THOUGHT

God lovingly created you with unique abilities and a unique personality. So why be jealous of someone else's abilities? Instead, throw your energy into using what God has specially given to you. Then you will be more confident about who you are and about the things you can do that no one else can. Who knows—someone else might be wishing they had your gifts!

TODAY'S PLAN

Have you discovered the unique abilities God has given you? What might God want you to do with them?

WARNINGS

TODAY'S PROMISE

The laws of the LORD are true; each one is fair. They are more desirable than gold, even the finest gold. They are sweeter than honey, even honey dripping from the comb. They are a warning to your servant, a great reward for those who obey them.

—PSALM 19:9-11

TODAY'S THOUGHT

God's warnings are designed to protect you from the consequences of foolish actions. For example, God's warning to avoid sexual immorality will protect you from the possibility of contracting sexually transmitted diseases. Too often, though, we view his warnings as obstacles to our freedom. When we do, we are rebelling against the very things designed to save us. God's warnings are his way of trying to protect you from doing something you'll regret later.

TODAY'S PLAN

Do you think God's warnings prevent you from enjoying life, or do you see them as blessings that help you enjoy life more?

PROMISES OF GOD

TODAY'S PROMISE

God has given both his promise and his oath. These two things are unchangeable because it is impossible for God to lie. Therefore, we who have fled to him for refuge can have great confidence as we hold to the hope that lies before us. —HEBREWS 6:18

TODAY'S THOUGHT

The trustworthiness of God should give you comfort for the present and assurance for the future. When you are absolutely convinced that God is able to do everything he promises, the troubles of your life will be put in perspective.

TODAY'S PLAN

On a scale of one to ten, how confident are you in God's promises?

WAR

TODAY'S PROMISE

The LORD will mediate between peoples and will settle disputes between strong nations far away. They will hammer their swords into plowshares and their spears into pruning hooks. Nation will no longer fight against nation, nor train for war anymore.

—MICAH 4:3

TODAY'S THOUGHT

There will come a day—the day Jesus returns—when war will be abolished forever. Imagine living in a world with no more fighting, violence, or bloodshed. This promise brings great comfort and joy, for you know that your eternal future will be one of lasting peace.

TODAY'S PLAN

Can you imagine a world without war?

SEPTEMBER

LISTENING

TODAY'S PROMISE

*Pay attention to how you hear. To those who listen
to my teaching, more understanding will be given.
But for those who are not listening, even what they
think they understand will be taken away from
them.*   —LUKE 8:18

TODAY'S THOUGHT

Always pay attention to the many ways in which
God speaks to you. Don't miss an opportunity
to learn a lesson from the Teacher. The more
you listen to God, the more you will understand. But if you close your ears and your heart
to him, even what you think you know will eventually prove to be nothing. You can listen to
God by reading the Bible, spending time in
prayer, and seeking wise advice from mature
Christians who have already learned how to
hear God.

TODAY'S PLAN

How can you learn to listen to God?

TEMPTATION

TODAY'S PROMISE

All glory to God, who is able to keep you from falling away and will bring you with great joy into his glorious presence without a single fault. All glory to him who alone is God, our Savior through Jesus Christ our Lord. —JUDE 1:24-25

TODAY'S THOUGHT

Everyone goes through times of temptation. How you deal with temptation determines whether or not you fall into sin. Your ability to resist temptation depends on your relationship with God. When God is your top priority, you are close enough to him that he is able to keep you from giving in to temptation and falling away from him.

TODAY'S PLAN

When you face temptations, do you always see a way out? Your answer reveals a lot about your relationship with God.

OBEDIENCE

TODAY'S PROMISE

If you love me, obey my commandments. And I will ask the Father, and he will give you another Advocate, who will never leave you. He is the Holy Spirit, who leads into all truth. —JOHN 14:15-17

TODAY'S THOUGHT

God promises to give you his own Holy Spirit, who is also called Advocate, or Counselor. As your counselor, the Spirit comes alongside you not only to advise and inspire you but to actually live and work within you. Just as the air you breathe is necessary for your body to work, so the Holy Spirit's power is necessary for you to obey God's commandments.

TODAY'S PLAN

How does the Holy Spirit empower you to obey?

OPPORTUNITIES

TODAY'S PROMISE

Keep watch and pray, so that you will not give in to temptation. For the spirit is willing, but the body is weak!

—MATTHEW 26:40-41

TODAY'S THOUGHT

Pray that God will prepare you to recognize and respond to good opportunities when they come and to avoid bad opportunities that might entice you. Prayer is a good way to stay alert and on the lookout for how God wants to work in your life. It keeps you connected to God and sensitive to his leading so you can better hear his voice and recognize when he is calling you to do something. When you rely on yourself, you miss out on a lot; when God connects with your spirit, you hear and see so much more.

TODAY'S PLAN

Are you staying well connected to God so you can take advantage of the opportunities he sends you?

CONVICTIONS

TODAY'S PROMISE

Let the Holy Spirit guide your lives. Then you won't be doing what your sinful nature craves. The sinful nature wants to do evil, which is just the opposite of what the Spirit wants. And the Spirit gives us desires that are the opposite of what the sinful nature desires. These two forces are constantly fighting each other, so you are not free to carry out your good intentions. —GALATIANS 5:16-17

TODAY'S THOUGHT

Every day you are faced with deciding between right and wrong, good and bad, God's way or the way of the world. It takes convictions to choose God's way, and it takes practice to keep your convictions strong. Don't let Satan take over any territory in your heart. Be committed to winning even the smaller battles. God promises you can do these things with the help of his Holy Spirit.

TODAY'S PLAN

What can you do today to develop stronger convictions?

POWER OF GOD

TODAY'S PROMISE

[Jesus] rebuked the wind and the raging waves. The storm stopped and all was calm. . . . The disciples were terrified and amazed. "Who is this man?" they asked each other. "When he gives a command, even the wind and waves obey him!" —LUKE 8:24-25

TODAY'S THOUGHT

The same Jesus who instantly calmed the storm over the Sea of Galilee has the power to calm the storms in your heart, to dry up any flood of fear, to banish any hunger for sin, and to control the whirlwinds of your life. Whether your life has changed dramatically since you became a Christian or you've had a quiet, steady walk of faith since childhood, your life can be a living demonstration of God's power at work within you.

TODAY'S PLAN

What can you tell others about the power of God at work in your life?

INFLUENCE

TODAY'S PROMISE

You are the salt of the earth. But what good is salt if it has lost its flavor?
                                                    —MATTHEW 5:13

TODAY'S THOUGHT

In Jesus' day, salt was an extremely valuable commodity. It was used as a seasoning and as a preservative to keep meat from spoiling. Jesus compares his followers to salt because they are to have a preservative effect on the world around them. When you keep your hearts holy and pure and hold up the standards of living found in God's Word, you help preserve the world from total decay.

TODAY'S PLAN

How "salty" is your life as a follower of Jesus? Do your words and actions help preserve others from going bad?

CHANGE

TODAY'S PROMISE

You, O God, are my refuge, the God who shows me unfailing love. —PSALM 59:17

TODAY'S THOUGHT

The character of God is unchanging and thus completely reliable. No matter how much your life changes, no matter what new situations you face, God goes with you. You can always count on his promise to help, to guide, and to care for you.

TODAY'S PLAN

When change moves you from one place to another, God is already there to welcome you. How can you learn to see him?

PRAYER

TODAY'S PROMISE

You are helping us by praying for us. Then many people will give thanks because God has graciously answered so many prayers. —2 CORINTHIANS 1:11

The earnest prayer of a righteous person has great power and produces wonderful results. —JAMES 5:16

TODAY'S THOUGHT

The Bible promises that praying for others makes a difference. It is easy to become discouraged if you think there is nothing anyone can do to help you with a particular problem—or nothing you can do to help someone else who needs it. But the most important thing you can do for others and that others can do for you is to pray. In ways beyond our understanding, prayer opens the door for the love and power of God to come through. Praying for others also causes you to care more about them.

TODAY'S PLAN

Who can you pray for today?

SALVATION

TODAY'S PROMISE

Because of Christ and our faith in him, we can now come boldly and confidently into God's presence.

—EPHESIANS 3:12

TODAY'S THOUGHT

If someone gave you a free pass to a concert or sports event, you wouldn't hesitate to go. You would have the privilege of admission because of the generosity of the giver. Your faith in Jesus Christ is God's free pass into his presence. When you put your trust in Jesus, you can enter God's presence with confidence.

TODAY'S PLAN

Have you accepted God's free pass to come into his presence?

ADVERSITY

TODAY'S PROMISE

When you go through deep waters, I will be with you. When you go through rivers of difficulty, you will not drown. When you walk through the fire of oppression, you will not be burned up; the flames will not consume you. For I am the LORD, your God, the Holy One of Israel, your Savior.

—ISAIAH 43:2-3

TODAY'S THOUGHT

When you are faced with great adversity, you may ask, "Where is God now, when I need him most?" The answer is always the same—he is right beside you. God is there, and he has the power to help you cope. God doesn't promise to save you from trouble in this life. God is not like a genie in a bottle, granting your every wish. Instead, God promises to be with you in your troubles and give you endurance to cope, as you learn to deal with adversity.

TODAY'S PLAN

When troubles overwhelm you, focus on how God will help you through them instead of how to escape them.

HURT

TODAY'S PROMISE

The LORD is close to the brokenhearted; he rescues those whose spirits are crushed. —PSALM 34:18

God blesses those who mourn, for they will be comforted. —MATTHEW 5:4

TODAY'S THOUGHT

Jesus suffered as much as any other human being. Because he can relate to your pain and because of his great love for you, God understands and cares when you are hurting. His heart breaks when yours is broken. He is with you in your pain, and he promises to bless you in the middle of it. Look for an extra measure of comfort from God; he will give it if you accept it.

TODAY'S PLAN

How often do you invite Jesus into your hurt?

DECISIONS

TODAY'S PROMISE

Your laws . . . give me wise advice. —PSALM 119:24

TODAY'S THOUGHT

Knowing the Bible and gleaning its wisdom gives you more options in your decision making and provides you with the discernment you need to make the best choices. A good decision is one that is consistent with the principles found in God's Word. If only one of the options you are deciding between would please God, then that is the right decision. If there are several options that are consistent with God's Word, then the process of trusting God to help you make the most of the path you choose may be more important than the decision itself.

TODAY'S PLAN

How can you look to the Bible for help with the decisions you're facing right now?

ANSWERS

TODAY'S PROMISE

Someone may say to you, "Let's ask the mediums and those who consult the spirits of the dead. With their whisperings and mutterings, they will tell us what to do." But shouldn't people ask God for guidance? Should the living seek guidance from the dead? Look to God's instructions and teachings!

—ISAIAH 8:19-20

TODAY'S THOUGHT

Only the God of the universe knows the answers to life's hardest questions. Don't trivialize God by believing that your life is nothing more than chance or by seeking answers from those who have only finite knowledge. Ask the God who has all the answers, and he will give you his truth and guidance.

TODAY'S PLAN

Do you turn to God for answers to your toughest questions?

HONESTY

TODAY'S PROMISE

The LORD detests the use of dishonest scales, but he delights in accurate weights. —PROVERBS 11:1

TODAY'S THOUGHT

If you want God's blessing, you must live by his standards of fairness and justice. Cheating is the opposite of honesty. The motive behind it is always to deceive someone else. God is delighted with people who are honest. He blesses those who show fairness and integrity.

TODAY'S PLAN

In what situations do you need to practice more honesty?

SALVATION

TODAY'S PROMISE

Since our friendship with God was restored by the death of his Son while we were still his enemies, we will certainly be saved through the life of his Son.

—ROMANS 5:10

TODAY'S THOUGHT

Sin separates you from God. That is why God sent his Son, Jesus, to die in your place. He took the punishment for your sins so you wouldn't have to. Jesus' resurrection from the dead proves his power over death and sin and gives you complete assurance that you will have eternal life with him. When you believe that Jesus died for your sins and was raised from the dead, when you confess your sins and ask God to forgive you, and when you commit yourself to obeying him, God gives you his salvation and restores you to fellowship with him both now and forever.

TODAY'S PLAN

Are you living as if you've been restored to fellowship with God?

EXAMPLE

TODAY'S PROMISE

Take a new grip with your tired hands and strengthen your weak knees. Mark out a straight path for your feet so that those who are weak and lame will not fall but become strong.

—HEBREWS 12:12-13

TODAY'S THOUGHT

Everyone is an example of something to someone else. We all follow the example of others, and we all set an example for others. The Bible promises that the way you live influences other people, and not just in matters of daily living; you can influence others for good or evil, for Christ or Satan. What kind of example have you been demonstrating lately to others?

TODAY'S PLAN

Do your words and actions set an example that leads others to be more like God?

NEIGHBOR

TODAY'S PROMISE

A second [commandment] is equally important: "Love your neighbor as yourself." —MATTHEW 22:39

If you love your neighbor, you will fulfill the requirements of God's law. —ROMANS 13:8

TODAY'S THOUGHT

Jesus taught that loving your neighbor as yourself is the second-greatest commandment. Why? Because God knows that human instinct is to take care of yourself first. But if you can train yourself to give equal priority to meeting the needs of others as well as your own needs, then you will know what love is all about. If you truly love others the way God intended, you will naturally carry out God's other instructions for service. Love directed inward has nowhere to go; love directed outward can change the world one person at a time.

TODAY'S PLAN

How well are you loving your friends, classmates, or teammates?

AVOIDANCE

TODAY'S PROMISE

When the teachers of religious law who were Pharisees saw him eating with tax collectors and other sinners, they asked his disciples, "Why does he eat with such scum?" When Jesus heard this, he told them, "Healthy people don't need a doctor—sick people do. I have come to call not those who think they are righteous, but those who know they are sinners."

—MARK 2:16-17

TODAY'S THOUGHT

As Christians, we are called to have relationships with unbelievers, not to avoid them. Doctors don't avoid the sick; they treat them. Those who don't know the saving power of Jesus are spiritually sick. If you avoid them, they might never realize that there is another way, a better way. Your relationship with an unbeliever might be the only way he or she will ever hear about God.

TODAY'S PLAN

Do you avoid those who don't know God or try to befriend them?

LIMITATIONS

TODAY'S PROMISE

It was to us that God revealed these things by his Spirit. For his Spirit searches out everything and shows us God's deep secrets. —1 CORINTHIANS 2:10

TODAY'S THOUGHT

Despite your human limitations, you can know the very thoughts of God because you have the Holy Spirit within you. The Bible tells us that God reveals spiritual truths to us that we could not understand without the help of the Holy Spirit. The next time life makes you aware of your limitations, don't be discouraged; instead, see it as an opportunity for God to reveal to you unique spiritual help that you could never get anywhere else.

TODAY'S PLAN

What spiritual truths has God been revealing to you?

BIBLE

TODAY'S PROMISE

All Scripture is inspired by God and is useful to teach us what is true and to make us realize what is wrong in our lives. It corrects us when we are wrong and teaches us to do what is right. God uses it to prepare and equip his people to do every good work.
—2 TIMOTHY 3:16-17

TODAY'S THOUGHT

If you buy a new computer but neglect to read the instruction manual, you'll miss out on many of the functions the machine is capable of doing. You'll be operating with just enough knowledge to perform basic functions. When it comes to reading the Bible, most of us read just enough to get by. We miss so much of what God's Word has to offer. Study the Bible daily so you can thoroughly understand everything God wants you to know. Then you will be able to live at peak performance.

TODAY'S PLAN

What can you do to develop the habit of studying God's Word?

LOVE

TODAY'S PROMISE

Hatred stirs up quarrels, but love makes up for all offenses. —PROVERBS 10:12

Love is patient and kind. Love is not jealous or boastful or proud or rude. It does not demand its own way. It is not irritable, and it keeps no record of being wronged. —1 CORINTHIANS 13:4-5

TODAY'S THOUGHT

Unconditional love means loving someone and doing the right thing even when the person you love hurts you. God shows us unconditional love, but consistently demonstrating that kind of love to others is perhaps the hardest thing for human beings to do. Unconditional love is the only way to experience meaningful and fulfilling relationships, and it is the only way to win over someone's heart.

TODAY'S PLAN

Do you know someone who needs to experience unconditional love? What conditions have you been putting on your most important relationships?

OUTSIDER

TODAY'S PROMISE

What blessings await you when people hate you and exclude you and mock you and curse you as evil because you follow the Son of Man. —LUKE 6:22

TODAY'S THOUGHT

Sometimes you might feel like an outsider because of your faith. In fact, you should feel that way because your real home is in heaven. Heaven is the place you were created for. Don't compromise your heavenly citizenship just to be with the in crowd here on earth. Instead, ask God to guide you to other believers with whom you can find fellowship and to unbelievers who need to know that there is something to look forward to beyond this life.

TODAY'S PLAN

You may feel like an outsider now, but you will be included in God's family for eternity. Does remembering that this life is temporary bring you comfort?

AUTHORITY

TODAY'S PROMISE

You say, "I am allowed to do anything"—but not everything is good for you. And even though "I am allowed to do anything," I must not become a slave to anything. . . . God bought you with a high price. So you must honor God with your body.

—1 CORINTHIANS 6:12, 20

TODAY'S THOUGHT

Authority is not always a bad thing; the abuse of authority is a bad thing. God's authority will not only save your life but will show you how to be successful and blessed. Don't rebel against that authority and jeopardize your soul. Rebelling against authority isn't the same thing as being able to be your own person. And being your own person doesn't mean doing whatever you want; it means using your God-given personality and talents to do what God wants.

TODAY'S PLAN

How can you be your own person for the glory of God?

WISDOM

TODAY'S PROMISE

Fear of the LORD is the foundation of true wisdom. All who obey his commandments will grow in wisdom.
                                                        —PSALM 111:10

TODAY'S THOUGHT

Although wisdom is often associated with the life experience that comes with age, God's wisdom is available to all of his children, regardless of age. There are wise young people and foolish older people. The key to having wisdom at any age is knowing and obeying God's commandments.

TODAY'S PLAN

Do you want to become wise beyond your years? Commit to studying and obeying God's commands in the Bible.

FRIENDSHIP

TODAY'S PROMISE

The LORD is a friend to those who fear him. He teaches them his covenant. —PSALM 25:14

TODAY'S THOUGHT

It may seem strange to think of being friends with the God of the universe, especially since you can't see or touch him. Think about the things that make your other friendships strong: trust, spending time together, communication, honesty, loyalty. Friendship with God isn't much different; it involves the same things. God has already offered his friendship to you. You can be friends with him if you truly seek him, walk with him, and love him.

TODAY'S PLAN

Are you developing a friendship with God?

FAILURE

TODAY'S PROMISE

This High Priest of ours understands our weaknesses, for he faced all of the same testings we do, yet he did not sin. So let us come boldly to the throne of our gracious God. There we will receive his mercy, and we will find grace to help us when we need it most. —HEBREWS 4:15-16

TODAY'S THOUGHT

God's work in your life is not limited by your failures. He doesn't reject you in your weakness; instead, he embraces you and strengthens you to be everything he created you to be. The seeds of success are often planted in the soil of failure.

TODAY'S PLAN

Do you feel like a failure? Have you asked God to turn your failure into his success?

POPULARITY

TODAY'S PROMISE

Many who are the greatest now will be least important then, and those who seem least important now will be the greatest then. —MATTHEW 19:30

TODAY'S THOUGHT

It's not wrong to want others to like you; it's a natural human desire. The problem comes when you are willing to do something wrong or compromise yourself in order to get other people's attention. Popularity is fleeting; the person who was popular yesterday is soon replaced by someone who seems cooler or funnier. Jesus saw this firsthand during the last week of his life on earth. The crowds who adored him on Palm Sunday called for his crucifixion on Good Friday. Instead of worrying about what others think of you, honor God and show love to everyone. You will be far more content, and others will admire you for it.

TODAY'S PLAN

Is your goal to honor God and others or to promote your own social status?

PASSION

TODAY'S PROMISE

I will give them singleness of heart and put a new spirit within them. I will take away their stony, stubborn heart and give them a tender, responsive heart.
—EZEKIEL 11:19

Joyful are those who obey his laws and search for him with all their hearts.
—PSALM 119:2

TODAY'S THOUGHT

If you become excited about something that is not what God wants you to do, your passion for God will quickly die. Sin takes your focus off God and makes it more exciting to pursue something else. Something besides God suddenly gets your attention. The solution to keeping your passion strong is to obey God's commands even when you don't feel like it. This may take a tremendous effort, but intense focus will keep you from becoming apathetic.

TODAY'S PLAN

Has anything become more exciting to you than following God? How can you renew your passion for him?

OCTOBER

HUMILIATION

TODAY'S PROMISE

Though your sins are like scarlet, I will make them as white as snow. Though they are red like crimson, I will make them as white as wool. —ISAIAH 1:18

TODAY'S THOUGHT

You can usually recover quickly from embarrassment, but it often takes much longer to recover from humiliation. If you experience humiliation, you can be out of commission for a long time. No one likes to be humiliated, but it can become a wonderful spiritual opportunity. It can lead you to repentance and restoration if it causes you to go to the only One who can forgive you and restore your reputation. God promises to make you as clean as newly fallen snow and turn your humiliation into an opportunity to experience his love and restoration.

TODAY'S PLAN

Are you involved in anything that could cause you humiliation if others found out about it?

LEARNING

TODAY'S PROMISE

Cry out for insight, and ask for understanding. Search for them as you would for silver; seek them like hidden treasures. Then you will understand what it means to fear the LORD, and you will gain knowledge of God. —PROVERBS 2:3-5

TODAY'S THOUGHT

If you've never thought of school as a place where you can learn about God, think again! The knowledge you gain at school might be God's way of preparing you for something in your future, something you have yet to discover. Often God shows you what to do as you make use of the opportunities—and classes!—he puts in your path. Make the most of where you are right now so you can make the most of where God will place you in the future.

TODAY'S PLAN

Are you learning things right now that don't seem relevant? How might these things be just what God wants you to learn to prepare you for your future?

IMPOSSIBLE

TODAY'S PROMISE

You faithfully answer our prayers with awesome deeds, O God our savior. You are the hope of everyone on earth, even those who sail on distant seas.

—PSALM 65:5

TODAY'S THOUGHT

While impossible situations seem to limit people and exhaust all human resources, they set the stage for God to do his best work—loving us, transforming bad into good and hurt into healing, bringing us salvation, changing lives, and meeting needs.

TODAY'S PLAN

What impossible situations are you facing? Are you watching for God to act on your behalf?

RECOGNITION

TODAY'S PROMISE

The gatekeeper opens the gate for him, and the sheep recognize his voice and come to him. He calls his own sheep by name and leads them out. After he has gathered his own flock, he walks ahead of them, and they follow him because they know his voice. They won't follow a stranger; they will run from him because they don't know his voice.

—JOHN 10:3-5

TODAY'S THOUGHT

When you really know someone, you can instantly recognize his or her voice. You can pick out a familiar voice in a crowd because it is distinct from the rest. In the same way, as you spend time studying the teachings of Jesus and getting to know him better through prayer, you will learn to recognize his voice. Then when you hear others preach or teach, you will be able to tell if what they are saying is consistent with what Jesus says.

TODAY'S PLAN

How well do you recognize the voice of Jesus?

OCTOBER 4

INJUSTICE

TODAY'S PROMISE

God is pleased with you when you do what you know is right and patiently endure unfair treatment.

—1 PETER 2:19

TODAY'S THOUGHT

Be willing to endure injustice in this life. Some things won't change until we get to heaven, where complete justice will finally be given out. If you are a victim of injustice, the real test is how you react to it. God promises to reward you if you patiently endure.

TODAY'S PLAN

How do you respond to a personal injustice?

HUMILITY

TODAY'S PROMISE

The high and lofty one who lives in eternity, the Holy One, says this: "I live in the high and holy place with those whose spirits are contrite and humble. I restore the crushed spirit of the humble and revive the courage of those with repentant hearts."
—ISAIAH 57:15

TODAY'S THOUGHT

God honors the humble and acknowledges their prayers. When you come to God in humility, your prayers are aligned with his will. You have taken the important step of recognizing that he is sovereign. He will lead you toward what is good and right, and away from sin and harm. After you fall to your knees in humility, you will be able to step out boldly in faith.

TODAY'S PLAN

Do you approach God in humility?

OCTOBER 6

LEADERSHIP

TODAY'S PROMISE

Among you it will be different. Whoever wants to be a leader among you must be your servant.

—MATTHEW 20:26

Even the Son of Man came not to be served but to serve others and to give his life as a ransom for many.

—MARK 10:45

TODAY'S THOUGHT

The biblical model for leadership is servant-hood. Worldly leaders use their power to do things for themselves, but godly leaders use their power to serve the people they are called to lead and care for. Worldly leaders want to be served; godly leaders want to serve. You may be in a position of leadership now, or you may someday become a leader wherever God places you. When you model the leadership style of Jesus, you will be a godly leader.

TODAY'S PLAN

What model of leadership do you want to follow?

MERCY

TODAY'S PROMISE

Great is his faithfulness; his mercies begin afresh each morning. —LAMENTATIONS 3:23

TODAY'S THOUGHT

We all long for a new start, a clean slate, a chance to begin again. Every day is a new start when it comes to God's mercy. Every day you can ask him to forgive your sins, and he will pour out his mercy on you, changing you from the inside out. When that happens, he no longer sees any sin in you. He doesn't see you as a failure; he sees you as his masterpiece. By God's grace and love, you are freed from the burdens of sin and failure so that you can have a fresh start, both in your eyes and his. To experience true life change, you must embrace God's life-changing mercy.

TODAY'S PLAN

Will you ask for God's mercy today?

TESTING

TODAY'S PROMISE

God blesses those who patiently endure testing and temptation. Afterward they will receive the crown of life that God has promised to those who love him. And remember, when you are being tempted, do not say, "God is tempting me." God is never tempted to do wrong, and he never tempts anyone else. —JAMES 1:12-13

TODAY'S THOUGHT

The Bible distinguishes between temptation, which Satan uses to lead you into sin, and testing, which God uses to purify you and help you grow and mature. Satan tempts you in order to destroy you. He wants you to fail and miss out on eternity with God. But God tests you for your own good. He wants you to succeed, both in this life and in eternity. He promises to reward you when you endure testing.

TODAY'S PLAN

Do you think God is testing you in some way? How might you grow stronger as you endure his testing?

FORGIVENESS

TODAY'S PROMISE

If you forgive those who sin against you, your heavenly Father will forgive you. But if you refuse to forgive others, your Father will not forgive your sins.

—MATTHEW 6:14-15

TODAY'S THOUGHT

Forgiveness is not an option; it is a command. Forgiveness is necessary for your relationship with God and your relationships with other people. Jesus gave you the perfect example of forgiveness. Forgiveness doesn't mean that your hurt doesn't exist or doesn't matter, nor does it make everything all right. Forgiveness allows you to let go of your hurt and let God deal with the one who hurt you. Forgiveness sets you free and allows you to move on with your life. It's not always easy, but forgiving someone who has hurt you is the best thing you can do for yourself.

TODAY'S PLAN

Are you modeling the forgiveness that God has shown you?

BROKENNESS

TODAY'S PROMISE

The sacrifice you desire is a broken spirit. You will not reject a broken and repentant heart, O God.

—PSALM 51:17

TODAY'S THOUGHT

God promises to draw close to you when you are brokenhearted over sin in your life. When you repent, you turn to God in brokenness over your sin. Then he begins to heal you and restore you.

TODAY'S PLAN

How often do you come to God with an attitude of brokenness over the sin in your life?

POWER OF GOD

TODAY'S PROMISE

It is not by force nor by strength, but by my Spirit, says the LORD of Heaven's Armies. —ZECHARIAH 4:6

TODAY'S THOUGHT

The Holy Spirit is the power of God that lives in every believer. When you yield control of your life to him, he releases his power within you— power to resist temptation, to serve and love God and others, to have wisdom in all circumstances, and to persevere in living for God here with the promise of eternal life in heaven. Through his Spirit, God will give you the power you need to do everything he asks you to do.

TODAY'S PLAN

How can you tap into God's power?

OCTOBER 12

PEACE

God blesses those who work for peace, for they will be called the children of God. —MATTHEW 5:9

TODAY'S THOUGHT

Sometimes your best response to opposition is no response at all. God isn't asking you to let yourself be pushed around by bullies, but he is asking you to oppose the right things. Most opposition only breeds confusion, conflict, and chaos. Working for peace fosters unity, harmony, and order. An environment of peace helps people get along, work together productively, and respect their differences. God promises to bless those who work for peace.

TODAY'S PLAN

Are you working for peace or contributing to the chaos?

WORK

TODAY'S PROMISE

Make it your goal to live a quiet life, minding your own business and working with your hands, just as we instructed you before. Then people who are not Christians will respect the way you live, and you will not need to depend on others.

—1 THESSALONIANS 4:11-12

TODAY'S THOUGHT

God promises two rewards for faithful work: (1) You become a witness to unbelievers, and (2) you don't have to be financially dependent on others. Whatever your job, there is immense dignity in all honest human labor, for your work is an opportunity to serve God and others. Believe that God has placed you in your position for a reason. Do your work to the best of your ability as a service to God until he opens another door of opportunity.

TODAY'S PLAN

Do you approach your work as a necessary evil or as an opportunity from God?

POVERTY

TODAY'S PROMISE

If you help the poor, you are lending to the LORD—and he will repay you!
—PROVERBS 19:17

TODAY'S THOUGHT

God has compassion for the poor and needy, so as a follower of God, you must also have compassion for them. Compassion that does not reach as far as your bank account or your to-do list is not godly compassion. Godly compassion requires action. Helping those less fortunate than you is not merely an obligation but a privilege that should bring you great joy.

TODAY'S PLAN

Do you know or know about someone who is poor? What can you do to help?

HIDING

TODAY'S PROMISE

If you search for him with all your heart and soul, you will find him. —DEUTERONOMY 4:29

TODAY'S THOUGHT

God wants you to know him, and he reveals himself to all those who seek him. Sometimes you may try to hide from God. You blame him when you feel far away from him. You claim that God is the one playing hard to get. Perhaps you are hiding because finding God means your life will change radically. But God is always trying to show himself to you. The question is, do you really want to find him? He promises to be found when you seek him wholeheartedly. Don't worry about what he might find in your heart; his desire is to help and heal you, not condemn you.

TODAY'S PLAN

Are you hiding from God? Begin seeking him today.

GUIDANCE

TODAY'S PROMISE

The LORD directs the steps of the godly. He delights in every detail of their lives. Though they stumble, they will never fall, for the LORD holds them by the hand.
—PSALM 37:23-24

TODAY'S THOUGHT

You are not irrelevant—you *can* make a difference in the world. The kind of choices you make determine whether or not you are participating in God's will. God's work will be accomplished—if not by you, then by someone else. If you want to participate in God's will, don't just sit around waiting for him to write a message on the wall. Seek his guidance first, and then make a decision to move ahead. When your decision making involves asking God for guidance, the choices you make will usually be in line with his will and you will be involved in his work.

TODAY'S PLAN

How can you seek God's guidance today and step out in faith to do what he asks?

TEMPER

TODAY'S PROMISE

People with understanding control their anger; a hot temper shows great foolishness. —PROVERBS 14:29

An angry person starts fights; a hot-tempered person commits all kinds of sin. —PROVERBS 29:22

TODAY'S THOUGHT

A short temper will get you in trouble. The more aggravated you get, the more angry you become, until finally you lash out in a fit of temper. When you feel the anger rising inside of you, train yourself to step away for a moment so you can cool off and think before you lash out. It may be hard to put into practice, but showing kindness and forgiveness will melt your anger away and keep your temper in check. As you grow toward spiritual maturity, you will learn to put your emotions under the control of the Holy Spirit.

TODAY'S PLAN

What kinds of situations cause anger to simmer inside of you? How can you keep your temper from flaring up?

WILL OF GOD

TODAY'S PROMISE

You see me when I travel and when I rest at home.
You know everything I do. —PSALM 139:3

TODAY'S THOUGHT

God created each of us for a specific purpose
and calls each of us to do specific tasks. As you
wait for God to reveal his specific will for you,
you can begin by carrying out what he wills for
every person—to love others and obey his Word.
Then you can be sure that you won't miss God's
will for you because you'll be living it every day.
When you arrive in heaven, it won't really matter what kind of grades, friends, clothes, car, or
job you had; what *will* matter is what kind of heart
you had. Were you faithful? Did you love others
and try to know God deeply? God is interested and involved in the details of your
life, but his primary will for all people is
simple obedience.

TODAY'S PLAN

What act of simple obedience can you do today?

OPPORTUNITIES

TODAY'S PROMISE

I know all the things you do, and I have opened a door for you that no one can close. —REVELATION 3:8

TODAY'S THOUGHT

You can trust that God knows your abilities. He places specific opportunities before you and gives you the tools you need to accept and fulfill them. When God opens a door, it will stay open as long as he wants; no person can close it. But you must walk through the open door!

TODAY'S PLAN

What door of opportunity has God opened for you recently? Have you walked through it yet?

BITTERNESS

TODAY'S PROMISE

Get rid of all bitterness, rage, anger, harsh words, and slander, as well as all types of evil behavior. Instead, be kind to each other, tenderhearted, forgiving one another, just as God through Christ has forgiven you.　　—EPHESIANS 4:31-32

TODAY'S THOUGHT

When someone hurts you, time will either harden your heart, making you bitter and unyielding, or soften it, giving you a desire to restore the relationship. When Jesus was asked how many times we should forgive others, he said "seventy times seven" (Matthew 18:22). Perhaps he meant that a never-ending willingness to forgive is the only way to mend a bitter spirit and heal broken relationships.

TODAY'S PLAN

Has someone hurt you recently? Is your heart growing hard, or are you willing to forgive for the sake of peace?

PRESENCE OF GOD

TODAY'S PROMISE

Nothing evil will be allowed to enter, nor anyone who practices shameful idolatry and dishonesty—but only those whose names are written in the Lamb's Book of Life.
—REVELATION 21:27

TODAY'S THOUGHT

Sin keeps you from fully enjoying God's presence because sin separates you from God, who is completely holy. Having your sin forgiven allows you to enter into God's presence. One day you will experience the complete wonder and intimacy of his presence in heaven when you see him face-to-face and he reads your name in the Book of Life.

TODAY'S PLAN

Is your name written in the Book of Life?

OVERWHELMED

The LORD always keeps his promises; he is gracious in all he does. The LORD helps the fallen and lifts those bent beneath their loads. The eyes of all look to you in hope. . . . The LORD is close to all who call on him, yes, to all who call on him in truth.

—PSALM 145:13-15, 18

TODAY'S THOUGHT

God loves to help those who are overwhelmed by life's troubles. He loves to pick up those who have tripped and fallen. When your life becomes more than you can bear, where do you go for help? God is waiting to reach down and pick you up. He may not eliminate all your problems, but he will help you see your way through your problems, and he promises to comfort you in the middle of them.

TODAY'S PLAN

Do you turn to God for help when you are overwhelmed by life?

GOD'S PROMISES

TODAY'S PROMISE

Because of his glory and excellence, he has given us great and precious promises. These are the promises that enable you to share his divine nature and escape the world's corruption caused by human desires.

—2 PETER 1:4

All this will happen if you carefully obey what the LORD your God says. —ZECHARIAH 6:15

TODAY'S THOUGHT

God's promises should motivate you to obey his commands because obeying God lets you share in all of his promises! God's promises of salvation and eternal life are only for those who believe in him, trust him, and commit to following him.

TODAY'S PLAN

Are you sharing in God's greatest promises?

GUIDANCE

TODAY'S PROMISE

The LORD is God, and he created the heavens and earth and put everything in place. He made the world to be lived in, not to be a place of empty chaos. "I am the LORD," he says, "and there is no other."

—ISAIAH 45:18

TODAY'S THOUGHT

While it may seem that some things just happen, much of what determines the direction of your life is part of God's plan for you. If everything happens merely by chance, then either there is no God at all, or God is impersonal and detached from the human race. But the Bible says that not only is God real, he is also compassionate and deeply involved in his creation. You may not understand how certain events in your life fit into God's perfect plan, but you can be confident that God is watching over you and guiding you in a specific direction. Will you follow where he leads?

TODAY'S PLAN

How can you recognize the doors of opportunity God opens for you today?

WITNESSING

TODAY'S PROMISE

Jesus called out to them, "Come, follow me, and I will show you how to fish for people!" —MARK 1:17

TODAY'S THOUGHT

Sharing your faith with others is a natural expression of your relationship with Jesus. Pray that God will give you spiritual sensitivity and the words to say. He promises to lead you to those he has made ready to hear his Good News.

TODAY'S PLAN

How can you learn to recognize the people God has placed in your path because they are ready to hear his Good News?

SPIRITUAL WARFARE

TODAY'S PROMISE

*Put on all of God's armor so that you will be able
to stand firm against all strategies of the devil.*

—EPHESIANS 6:11

TODAY'S THOUGHT

Your best offensive weapon in spiritual warfare
is the Word of God. It's odd to think of the Bible
as a weapon, but in it God reveals his plan of
attack against the forces of evil that try to bring
you down. If you don't read it, you won't know
how to fight the battle that literally determines
your destiny, both here on earth and in heaven
for eternity. Only by knowing whom you are
fighting, where the battle is being fought, and
how to defend yourself will you be able to win.
It is vital to study God's Word as much as you
can. This weapon will send Satan running
for cover.

TODAY'S PLAN

How often are you using your best offensive weapon?

TEAMWORK

TODAY'S PROMISE

Two people are better off than one, for they can help each other succeed.
—ECCLESIASTES 4:9

TODAY'S THOUGHT

Accomplishments can be multiplied through teamwork. It is impossible for one person to create the harmony of a duet or a trio. You can't play a team sport like football or soccer without teamwork. It is hard to have a strong friendship if only one person works at it. That's why the Bible teaches that two people working together can do much more than one, as long as they are pulling in the same direction.

TODAY'S PLAN

Do you prefer to go it alone? How might you accomplish more through cooperation and teamwork?

BUSYNESS

TODAY'S PROMISE

Enthusiasm without knowledge is no good; haste makes mistakes. —PROVERBS 19:2

TODAY'S THOUGHT

Don't confuse busyness with accomplishment. A schedule that is too full may reflect a lack of wise priorities. If you are too busy, you won't have time to do anything well, to learn more, or to grow deeper in your faith. Activity without real purpose will cause you to make mistakes and will leave you feeling empty and worn out.

TODAY'S PLAN

Are you trying to do too much? Figure out what God wants you to do—that's enough!

INTEGRITY

TODAY'S PROMISE

The LORD rewarded me for doing right. He has seen my innocence. To the faithful you show yourself faithful; to those with integrity you show integrity.

—PSALM 18:24-25

TODAY'S THOUGHT

If you want to be used by God, you must commit yourself to a life of integrity. Integrity begins with the small choices you make when no one else is watching; it blossoms into the guiding principle of your life and your relationships when you have complete consistency between your beliefs and your behavior. God promises to faithfully reward you when you faithfully do the right thing.

TODAY'S PLAN

What steps can you take to develop the kind of integrity God rewards?

SATAN

TODAY'S PROMISE

Humble yourselves before God. Resist the devil, and he will flee from you.
— JAMES 4:7

TODAY'S THOUGHT

Satan's greatest goal is to get God's followers to do anything that does not involve God. He will try to get you to ignore God, forget about God, be apathetic about God, deny God, doubt God, and sin against God. And he's working full-time to accomplish his goal. If you give in even a little, he'll just attack you harder. But if you ignore Satan, neglect him, fight him, deny him, and resist him, eventually he will go bother someone else, someone who's an easier target. He will flee from you if he gets the clear message that he cannot win you over.

TODAY'S PLAN

How can you increase your resistance so Satan will leave you alone?

HELL

TODAY'S PROMISE

You can enter God's Kingdom only through the narrow gate. The highway to hell is broad, and its gate is wide for the many who choose that way.

—MATTHEW 7:13

TODAY'S THOUGHT

The greatest misconception people have about hell is that it doesn't exist. Just as we believe scientists when they tell us gravity exists, we should believe God when he tells us hell exists. Many people wonder how a merciful and loving God could send people to such a terrible place. The truth is that God doesn't send anyone to hell; people choose to go there when they continually resist God, and God honors their choice. The only way to go to heaven instead of hell is to surrender to God. Then he forgives you and gives you eternal life in heaven. God doesn't want anyone to go to hell, but he respects us enough to let us choose.

TODAY'S PLAN

Do you believe what God's Word says about hell?

NOVEMBER

PRIORITIES

TODAY'S PROMISE

Jesus replied, "The most important commandment is this: . . . You must love the LORD your God with all your heart, all your soul, all your mind, and all your strength.' The second is equally important: 'Love your neighbor as yourself.' No other commandment is greater than these." —MARK 12:29-31

TODAY'S THOUGHT

Interruptions tend to become our top priorities. When the phone rings, most of us get up to answer it or at least check the caller ID. Our lives usually skip from one urgent interruption to another, and we keep missing what is really important. How can we determine what should be a high priority and what should be a low priority? Jesus clearly stated the two greatest priorities everyone should have: to love God and to love others, with everything we've got.

TODAY'S PLAN

Make a list of your top five priorities. Do you need to reevaluate them in light of God's greatest priorities?

INSTRUCTIONS FOR LIFE

TODAY'S PROMISE

The LORD grants wisdom! From his mouth come knowledge and understanding. —PROVERBS 2:6

TODAY'S THOUGHT

If you buy something labeled "Some assembly required" but you don't follow the instructions, what you assemble will not work properly. It's the same with life. When you follow God's instruction manual—the Bible—God promises that your life will work much better. God created life and established the rules that govern how it should work. Throughout the history of the world, people have done what was right in their own eyes and have experienced catastrophic consequences as a result. Your job is not to pass judgment on God's ways by devising your own but to follow God and his Word.

TODAY'S PLAN

Are you following the Bible's instructions for living? In what ways have you seen that they really work?

FULFILLMENT

TODAY'S PROMISE

When will you stop panting after other gods?

—JEREMIAH 2:25

[God] himself gives life and breath to everything, and he satisfies every need. —ACTS 17:25

TODAY'S THOUGHT

God wants you to enjoy many things. It is only when something becomes more important to you than God that you get into trouble. What do you spend most of your time chasing after—popularity, success, leisure, pleasure? Whatever it is, don't let it become your god. It is only when you chase after the one true God that you will find true fulfillment. Chasing other gods is a tiring business, and one pursuit after another ends in disappointment and dissatisfaction. Only God can fulfill your every need.

TODAY'S PLAN

What other gods have you been chasing after? How can you chase after the one true God and find ultimate fulfillment?

WORDS

TODAY'S PROMISE

Who may worship in your sanctuary, LORD?
Who may enter your presence on your holy hill?
Those who lead blameless lives and do what is right,
speaking the truth from sincere hearts. Those who
refuse to gossip or harm their neighbors or speak
evil of their friends. —PSALM 15:1-3

TODAY'S THOUGHT

You would never give an obscene gift to, say, the President, or even to a friend; you'd certainly never give an insulting gift to an enemy. Your words are no different. In fact, the greatest gift you can give others is not something in a box covered with paper and ribbons but in the words you speak to encourage, inspire, comfort, and challenge them. Don't let your words be annoying, insulting, demeaning, or simply useless. Make sure your words truly matter because they show the kind of person you are.

TODAY'S PLAN

If you were to keep separate lists of both the positive and negative words you speak today, which list would be longer?

SERVING

TODAY'S PROMISE

Well done, my good and faithful servant. You have been faithful in handling this small amount, so now I will give you many more responsibilities.

—MATTHEW 25:21

TODAY'S THOUGHT

Sometimes we fall into the habit of expecting others to take care of our needs while we wait for God to show us his will, but that causes us to focus inward on ourselves. As you wait, you should serve God and others because it is through serving that you will receive your next assignment from God. The servant in the parable was praised for serving while the master was gone. You can be confident that God wants you to faithfully serve him right where you are as you await your next instructions from him.

TODAY'S PLAN

How can you serve today while you wait to learn what God might call you to do tomorrow?

VALUE

TODAY'S PROMISE

God showed how much he loved us by sending his one and only Son into the world so that we might have eternal life through him. This is real love—not that we loved God, but that he loved us and sent his Son as a sacrifice to take away our sins.

—1 JOHN 4:9-10

TODAY'S THOUGHT

What makes something valuable? One way to determine the value of something is to consider the price that was paid for it. Other considerations of an object's value include its uniqueness and its purpose. When God created you, he uniquely designed you for a special purpose because he loves you and has a plan for you. Then he paid the ultimate price for you by sending his Son to die for you. You are immeasurably valuable to God. You are priceless!

TODAY'S PLAN

Can you grasp the enormous price God paid to have a relationship with you? How valuable does that make you feel?

PEACE

TODAY'S PROMISE

The LORD gives his people strength. The LORD blesses them with peace. —PSALM 29:11

TODAY'S THOUGHT

Faith in God brings peace of mind and heart because it links you to God's mind and heart. Knowing that God is sovereign gives you the peaceful assurance that he is in control.

TODAY'S PLAN

Are you looking in the right place for peace?

ENCOURAGEMENT

TODAY'S PROMISE

As soon as I pray, you answer me; you encourage me by giving me strength. —PSALM 138:3

TODAY'S THOUGHT

You can receive encouragement through an active prayer life. You have a supernatural connection when you talk with the Creator of the universe. What an encouragement to know that God answers your prayers and gives you strength! The act of prayer is a powerful reminder that your life is in the hands of a loving God who cares deeply about what happens to you.

TODAY'S PLAN

How have you been encouraged through prayer?

CARE

TODAY'S PROMISE

If God cares so wonderfully for wildflowers that are here today and thrown into the fire tomorrow, he will certainly care for you. Why do you have so little faith?
—MATTHEW 6:30

TODAY'S THOUGHT

God is always close to you, ready to take care of you in your time of need. God's presence surrounds you, protecting you from Satan's attacks. God sends opportunities your way to make your life more full and satisfying. He sends you countless blessings. He promises to take your worries and cares upon himself. And he offers you eternal life in heaven, away from all hurt, pain, and sin. These are just some of the ways God fulfills his promise to care for you.

TODAY'S PLAN

Make a list of how God has cared for you in the past. You will be amazed at how long it is!

GUIDANCE

TODAY'S PROMISE

The LORD says, "I will guide you along the best pathway for your life. I will advise you and watch over you."

—PSALM 32:8

TODAY'S THOUGHT

If we could see the future, we'd likely become scared of the hard times ahead or proud of our accomplishments. God's guidance is not like a searchlight that brightens a broad area; instead, it's more like a flashlight that illuminates just enough of the path ahead to show you where to take the next step. God has a definite plan for you, but he usually doesn't reveal it all at once. He wants you to learn to trust him each step of the way.

TODAY'S PLAN

How can you trust God's guidance today by taking one step forward?

TROUBLES

TODAY'S PROMISE

Don't let your hearts be troubled. Trust in God,
and trust also in me. . . . I am leaving you with a
gift—peace of mind and heart. And the peace I give
is a gift the world cannot give. So don't be troubled
or afraid.   —JOHN 14:1, 27

TODAY'S THOUGHT

Your troubles do not surprise God, and they
shouldn't surprise you. Trouble is a fact of life
in this fallen world. Try to look less at your
problems and more at Jesus, who experienced
all your troubles. He promises to show you how
to have peace in spite of them.

TODAY'S PLAN

How can you focus a little more on Jesus and a little less
on your problems today?

SUFFERING

TODAY'S PROMISE

By means of their suffering, he rescues those who suffer. For he gets their attention through adversity.

—JOB 36:15

Come back to the place of safety. . . . I promise this very day that I will repay two blessings for each of your troubles.

—ZECHARIAH 9:12

TODAY'S THOUGHT

Suffering is not a sign that God doesn't care. It is a universal experience, and God uses it to draw people to him. If God took away our suffering in this life, we would not need him or desire heaven. Perhaps we would only follow him to receive an instant cure rather than because of our need for salvation. While the Bible does not promise a life free from pain, it does promise that God is with you in your pain and that all of your troubles will end one day. God promises that his people will not have to suffer forever.

TODAY'S PLAN

Can you look beyond today's suffering and rejoice that God will one day take all of it away?

BETRAYAL

TODAY'S PROMISE

Everyone has sinned; we all fall short of God's glorious standard. Yet God, with undeserved kindness, declares that we are righteous. He did this through Christ Jesus when he freed us from the penalty for our sins. —ROMANS 3:23-24

TODAY'S THOUGHT

There is nothing more painful than betrayal, but you can't avoid betraying God. Every person has sinned and will continue to sin against God. But if you realize you are a sinner and confess your sins to God, he will forgive you. He will look at you and treat you as though you have never betrayed him. A God who promises to love you despite your betrayal is a God worth trusting and following.

TODAY'S PLAN

How have you betrayed God? If you ask him to forgive you, he will forget about it—forever.

PATIENCE

TODAY'S PROMISE

May God, who gives . . . patience and encouragement, help you live in complete harmony with each other, as is fitting for followers of Christ Jesus.
—ROMANS 15:5

TODAY'S THOUGHT

Patience leads to harmony with others, endurance to handle difficult circumstances, and an expectant attitude of hope that things will get better. It demonstrates a thoughtful attitude toward the feelings of others. Only God can give you the kind of patience that causes you to enjoy the process of learning how to get along with others. It may take time, but the rewards of living in harmony with your Christian brothers and sisters are deep and profound.

TODAY'S PLAN

Do you need more of God's patience to get along with the people around you?

NEEDS

TODAY'S PROMISE

Since he did not spare even his own Son but gave him up for us all, won't he also give us everything else?
—ROMANS 8:32

TODAY'S THOUGHT

There are some basic spiritual needs that God promises he will always meet. God will always meet your need for salvation, mercy, wisdom, comfort, strength, a way out of temptation, and faith. He meets these needs through the Holy Spirit living within you.

TODAY'S PLAN

Which of your needs do you most often ask God to meet? Are they the most important ones?

STEWARDSHIP

TODAY'S PROMISE

Whether we are here in this body or away from this body, our goal is to please him. For we must all stand before Christ to be judged. We will each receive whatever we deserve for the good or evil we have done in this earthly body. —2 CORINTHIANS 5:9-10

TODAY'S THOUGHT

The goal of stewardship is to make the best possible use of what you have in order to make the greatest possible impact on others so that God's work can move forward as efficiently and effectively as possible. You are ultimately accountable to God for how you use your gifts and opportunities, whether for yourself or for the benefit others. God entrusts you with certain resources and abilities and then expects you to maximize them through wise and godly stewardship. God promises to reward you if you use well what he has entrusted to you.

TODAY'S PLAN

Are you a good steward of the resources and abilities God has given you?

REMEMBERING

TODAY'S PROMISE

I recall all you have done, O LORD; I remember your wonderful deeds of long ago. They are constantly in my thoughts. I cannot stop thinking about your mighty works. O God, your ways are holy. Is there any god as mighty as you? You are the God of great wonders! —PSALM 77:11-14

TODAY'S THOUGHT

When you're in trouble, pray. When you can't sleep at night, pray. Pray with intensity. As you ask for God's help, remember the things he has already done for you, the answers to prayer he has given in the past, and the fact that he is the almighty God of miracles. Remember that he has helped you and other believers before, and he will surely help you again. Think about God's mighty works to restore your faith that he will listen to you and help you in your time of trouble.

TODAY'S PLAN

How can you remember to keep God constantly in your thoughts?

GOODNESS

TODAY'S PROMISE

A good person produces good things from the treasury of a good heart, and an evil person produces evil things from the treasury of an evil heart.

—MATTHEW 12:35

TODAY'S THOUGHT

What you say and do opens a window to your soul and shows everyone around you what is inside. If you practice the goodness you have received from God, others will see treasures within. If you don't, the bad things you say and do will reveal the impoverishment of your soul.

TODAY'S PLAN

Can others see a treasury of goodness inside of you?

FORGIVENESS

TODAY'S PROMISE

O LORD, you are so good, so ready to forgive, so full of unfailing love for all who ask for your help.

—PSALM 86:5

TODAY'S THOUGHT

No sin is so big or so terrible that God won't forgive it if you ask him. God has seen it all, and he still offers everyone his complete and unconditional love. But God does not force his forgiveness upon you. If you want it and ask for it, he will always give it. He wants a relationship with you, and it is only through his forgiveness of your sin that you can have a relationship with him. Only those who don't want God's forgiveness are beyond its reach.

TODAY'S PLAN

Have you asked for and accepted God's forgiveness?

BLESSINGS

TODAY'S PROMISE

How great is the goodness you have stored up for those who fear you. You lavish it on those who come to you for protection, blessing them before the watching world. —PSALM 31:19

TODAY'S THOUGHT

God's blessings come to you every day, in every conceivable form. Success and prosperity are not the most important blessings from God, for they tend to take our minds off of him. Rather, his presence, the beauty of creation, peace of mind and heart, joy, spiritual gifts, family, friends, comfort, and hope are some of the best blessings he gives. The greatest blessing God wants to give you is salvation and eternal life.

TODAY'S PLAN

Can you count the blessings God has given you? Which ones do you think are most important?

HURT

TODAY'S PROMISE

*He will swallow up death forever! The Sovereign
LORD will wipe away all tears.*   —ISAIAH 25:8

*Our present troubles are small and won't last very
long. Yet they produce for us a glory that vastly
outweighs them and will last forever!*

—2 CORINTHIANS 4:17

TODAY'S THOUGHT

God does not promise believers a life free from
pain and suffering. If Christians didn't hurt,
other people might see God only as some sort of
magician who takes away all the bad things in life.
But because you have a relationship with God,
he helps you, comforts you, and sometimes
miraculously heals your hurt. Most importantly, God will one day take away all of your
hurt when you arrive in heaven. Whatever
pain you are experiencing is only temporary.
Perhaps it will end here on earth, but you
can be certain there is no hurt in heaven.

TODAY'S PLAN

*Do you believe God's promise that he will turn your
present hurts into eternal joy?*

THANKFULNESS

TODAY'S PROMISE

Since everything God created is good, we should not reject any of it but receive it with thanks.

—1 TIMOTHY 4:4

TODAY'S THOUGHT

Cultivate thankfulness by regularly giving thanks to God, either alone or with others. Set aside time every day to meditate on the things you are thankful for. Make a mental list of God's blessings in your life, and thank him for them. Don't wait until you feel thankful before you give thanks. Giving thanks will lead you to feel thankful.

TODAY'S PLAN

Are you cultivating a thankful heart, toward God and toward others?

PRAISE

TODAY'S PROMISE

It is good to give thanks to the LORD, to sing praises to the Most High. —PSALM 92:1

TODAY'S THOUGHT

When you praise the Lord, it lifts your mood. It is a deliberate act of worship that is hard to do when you are feeling down, but it produces almost immediate results. Praise the Lord for his unfailing, unconditional love for you. Praise him for the gift of salvation and eternal life. Praise him for his promise to help you through your hard times. Praise him for anything good you see around you. Your praise will turn your attitude around.

TODAY'S PLAN

What can you praise God for right now?

NOVEMBER 24

HERITAGE

TODAY'S PROMISE

Because we are united with Christ, we have received an inheritance from God, . . . The Spirit is God's guarantee that he will give us the inheritance he promised and that he has purchased us to be his own people. —EPHESIANS 1:11, 14

TODAY'S THOUGHT

You can't choose the family you were born into, but you can choose a spiritual heritage by choosing to join the family of God. You can tap into the witness and wisdom of those who have faithfully served God in the past, as well as the very presence and power of God himself in the form of the Holy Spirit. All those who believe in Jesus Christ are God's children. If you love him, obey him, and worship him, he promises to give you an eternal inheritance.

TODAY'S PLAN

Regardless of your earthly heritage, have you received the spiritual heritage that comes from belonging to God's family?

THANKFULNESS

TODAY'S PROMISE

Giving thanks is a sacrifice that truly honors me. If you keep to my path, I will reveal to you the salvation of God. —PSALM 50:23

TODAY'S THOUGHT

When you give thanks to God, you honor and praise him for everything he has done—in your life, in the lives of others, in the church, in the world. Similarly, when you thank other people, you honor them and show them respect for who they are and what they have done. This attitude of gratitude helps you serve others and allows you to enjoy whatever blessings come your way.

TODAY'S PLAN

Are you becoming more or less thankful each day?

KINDNESS

TODAY'S PROMISE

The LORD is merciful and compassionate, slow to get angry and filled with unfailing love. . . . The LORD is righteous in everything he does; he is filled with kindness. —PSALM 145:8, 17

TODAY'S THOUGHT

God didn't just create kindness, he is kindness itself. He gives you mercy when you don't deserve it. He is patient with you instead of punishing you when you do something wrong. He loves you unconditionally. Everything God does for you is an act of kindness to help you become the person he created you to be.

TODAY'S PLAN

What acts of kindness has God shown to you lately? Take some time right now to make a list of them.

THANKFULNESS

TODAY'S PROMISE

Be thankful in all circumstances, for this is God's will for you who belong to Christ Jesus.

—1 THESSALONIANS 5:18

TODAY'S THOUGHT

Think about how often in a day others do something for you, however small. Do you remember to thank them? Now think about how often God helps you in your daily life. Think about how much God has given you. When you pause to thank God, you will see that he has a perfect track record of blessing you, providing for you, and protecting you. How often do you give thanks to him? Giving thanks is a way to celebrate both the giver and the gift. Remember to thank God in everything.

TODAY'S PLAN

How often do you thank God for the blessings in your life?

GREED

TODAY'S PROMISE

Don't store up treasures here on earth. . . . Store your treasures in heaven, where moths and rust cannot destroy, and thieves do not break in and steal. Wherever your treasure is, there the desires of your heart will also be. —MATTHEW 6:19-21

TODAY'S THOUGHT

How long do you want to enjoy the good things in life? If you're concerned only about the temporary pleasures that come from the things of this life here on earth, you're more likely to have a problem with greed. But if you'd like to enjoy heavenly treasures for eternity, then you're more likely to be generous. You will find yourself investing in different things today so that you can enjoy God's rewards forever.

TODAY'S PLAN

How can you develop more interest in eternal treasures rather than temporary ones?

COPING

TODAY'S PROMISE

The LORD helps the fallen and lifts those bent beneath their loads.   —PSALM 145:14

TODAY'S THOUGHT

Coping is the manner in which you deal with life. You can't control your circumstances, but you can control how you respond to them and whom you go to for help. You need the proper perspective to cope with life. God encourages you not to run away from your problems or try to escape them but to work through them. Then you will come out stronger on the other side. Through it all, God offers strength and wisdom that you cannot find anywhere else. How you respond to the challenges of life, including how much you rely on God, determines how well you cope.

TODAY'S PLAN

Are you coping with life from God's perspective?

APATHY

TODAY'S PROMISE

Don't look out only for your own interests, but take an interest in others, too. —PHILIPPIANS 2:4

*Keep on loving others as long as life lasts. . . .
Then you will not become spiritually dull and indifferent.* —HEBREWS 6:11-12

TODAY'S THOUGHT

The more interested you are in something, the less apathetic you will be. The more interested you are in the lives of those around you, the more you'll care about them. Getting involved in the lives of others will keep you from becoming dull and indifferent to their needs, and it will challenge you to think about ways to reflect God's love to them.

TODAY'S PLAN

How well do you really know the people in your life? Are you apathetic toward most of them or genuinely interested in their lives?

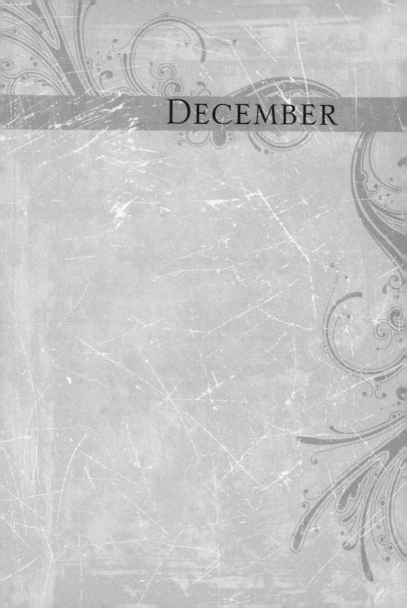

DECEMBER

REWARDS

If you give even a cup of cold water to one of the least of my followers, you will surely be rewarded.

—MATTHEW 10:42

Give, and you will receive.

—LUKE 6:38

TODAY'S THOUGHT

One of the unique promises of the Bible is that the more you give, the more you receive—not necessarily in material possessions, but in spiritual and eternal rewards. This is a truth that can be learned only by doing. Your monetary investments will become worthless to you when you die—you can't take them with you. But any spiritual investments you make will reward you with eternal payoffs.

TODAY'S PLAN

What can you give today that might be rewarded in heaven?

INTEGRITY

TODAY'S PROMISE

I will bring that group through the fire and make them pure. I will refine them like silver and purify them like gold. They will call on my name, and I will answer them. I will say, "These are my people," and they will say, "The LORD is our God."

—ZECHARIAH 13:9

TODAY'S THOUGHT

Integrity is essentially the correspondence between your character and the character of God. To develop integrity, your character must become more and more like God's. Just as pure gold is the result of a refining process that purifies the metal and tests it with fire, a life of integrity is the result of a refining process in which you are tested daily to see how pure you are. If God sees that your thoughts and actions are becoming increasingly pure through this testing, then your character is becoming more like his, and you are gradually gaining integrity.

TODAY'S PLAN

Is your character becoming more or less like God's each day?

RIGHTEOUSNESS

TODAY'S PROMISE

*The LORD . . . hears the prayers of the righteous.
. . . The godly run to him and are safe. . . . The
godly are as bold as lions.* —PROVERBS 15:29; 18:10; 28:1

*The righteous will shine like the sun in their
Father's Kingdom.* —MATTHEW 13:43

TODAY'S THOUGHT

Those who are righteous, or godly, in God's
eyes are safe in his care—their souls cannot be
snatched away by Satan; bold in his work—they
have the courage to do the right thing and are not
ashamed of their faith; persistent in prayer—they
enjoy close fellowship with God; and outwardly
radiant from inner beauty—others can see they
are different and are attracted to what they
see in them. God promises all these things
to you when you are righteous before him
through faith in his Son, Jesus.

TODAY'S PLAN

Does God consider you to be righteous?

GIVING

TODAY'S PROMISE

Yes, you will be enriched in every way so that you can always be generous. And when we take your gifts to those who need them, they will thank God. So two good things will result from this ministry of giving— the needs of the believers . . . will be met, and they will joyfully express their thanks to God. As a result . . . they will give glory to God.

—2 CORINTHIANS 9:11-13

TODAY'S THOUGHT

Giving gifts to God glorifies him. It enriches your life and the lives of others because both you and they will experience God's generosity and be fulfilled by God's blessings. Others will thank God and honor him as their needs are met, and they will be encouraged to continue the cycle of giving.

TODAY'S PLAN

Are you continuing the cycle of giving?

SHARING

TODAY'S PROMISE

This is what the LORD says: "Don't let the wise boast in their wisdom, or the powerful boast in their power, or the rich boast in their riches. But those who wish to boast should boast in this alone: that they truly know me and understand that I am the LORD who demonstrates unfailing love and who brings justice and righteousness to the earth, and that I delight in these things. I, the LORD, have spoken!" —JEREMIAH 9:23-24

TODAY'S THOUGHT

When you know God and understand how much he loves you, you will want to share his goodness with others. This is not bragging—it is sharing a wonderful secret that could change someone's life! So don't boast in your blessings, but share the blessings of God's love. Then you will enjoy his love even more.

TODAY'S PLAN

How can you share God's goodness with someone else today?

INTENTIONS

TODAY'S PROMISE

It is better to say nothing than to make a promise and not keep it. —ECCLESIASTES 5:5

TODAY'S THOUGHT

There are no rewards for good intentions. If you intend to become a Christian "someday" but never get around to it, you forfeit the reward of heaven. If you intend to thank someone for helping you but never get around to it, they may never know how you really feel about what they did for you. Good intentions require follow-through and perseverance to become reality and reap rewards.

TODAY'S PLAN

Do you have good intentions for your relationship with God that you have yet to follow through on?

HABITS

TODAY'S PROMISE

Those who are dominated by the sinful nature think about sinful things, ... Letting your sinful nature control your mind leads to death. But letting the Spirit control your mind leads to life and peace.

—ROMANS 8:5-6

TODAY'S THOUGHT

Bad habits are hard to break, and sinful habits are even harder. The sinful nature you inherited at birth is very powerful. It will dominate your thinking unless you have a greater power to defeat it. That greater power is God's Holy Spirit. If you've asked Jesus into your life, he has placed the Holy Spirit inside you. You are not strong enough to fight your sinful nature, but the Holy Spirit is. Let him control your heart and mind, and you will be able to get rid of your bad habits as well as your sinful ones.

TODAY'S PLAN

What are some habits you're trying to break? Have you asked for the Holy Spirit's help?

HEAVEN

TODAY'S PROMISE

We live with great expectation, and we have a priceless inheritance—an inheritance that is kept in heaven for you, pure and undefiled, beyond the reach of change and decay.
—1 PETER 1:3-4

TODAY'S THOUGHT

One of the greatest promises in the Bible is God's vow to forgive your sins and give you eternal life in heaven. You can be sure that this promise will be fulfilled because Jesus not only died on the cross to take the punishment for your sins but also rose from the dead. God promises that those who believe this will live forever with him in heaven, where there will be no pain, suffering, or evil. When you believe God's promises, you will have a life and a future that is far beyond anything you can imagine.

TODAY'S PLAN

Are you confident in God's promise of heaven?

ANGER

TODAY'S PROMISE

O God . . . Why have you forgotten me? Why must I wander around in grief, oppressed by my enemies?

—PSALM 42:9

Morning, noon, and night I cry out in my distress, and the LORD hears my voice.

—PSALM 55:17

TODAY'S THOUGHT

God wants you to be honest with him, even if you are angry with him. Any close relationship must include honesty, even if it reveals less-than-noble feelings. The truth is that you do sometimes get mad at God. Perhaps it's when you don't understand why God allows bad people to succeed or tragedies to occur. When you express your honest anger to the Lord, you express your faith that he hears you and has the power to help you.

TODAY'S PLAN

Are you angry at God? Honestly express your feelings to him, and he will listen.

PEACE

TODAY'S PROMISE

There will be glory and honor and peace from God for all who do good. —ROMANS 2:10

TODAY'S THOUGHT

Peace with God comes from living the way God wants you to live. That happens when you develop a relationship with him and live by the standards he has written in his Word, the Bible. Let go of a lifestyle of ignoring and neglecting God, and work toward living a life that honors and obeys him. You will experience God's peace when your mind, heart, and actions get in sync with his.

TODAY'S PLAN

How can you experience peace with God?

SUCCESS

TODAY'S PROMISE

What do you benefit if you gain the whole world but lose your own soul? Is anything worth more than your soul?
—MATTHEW 16:26

TODAY'S THOUGHT

When it comes to success, you must decide whose rules you want to play by. Would you rather be a success in school but a failure as a friend, or vice versa? Would you rather be a success in the world's eyes or in God's eyes? In reality, these are not necessarily mutually exclusive. But if you were given these choices, what you would decide? Now is the time to decide what definition of success you will live by. The Bible teaches you to define success in terms of faithfulness to God. That is the standard by which you must measure everything else. God will reward your faithfulness even if you fail in the eyes of the world.

TODAY'S PLAN

What standard of success are you living by?

TITHING

TODAY'S PROMISE

"Bring all the tithes into the storehouse so there will be enough food in my Temple. If you do," says the LORD of Heaven's Armies, "I will open the windows of heaven for you. I will pour out a blessing so great you won't have enough room to take it in! Try it! Put me to the test!" —MALACHI 3:10

TODAY'S THOUGHT

God wanted his people to tithe—to give him the first tenth of their income—to demonstrate their obedience and trust that he would provide for them. But tithing is still a good discipline because it shows your commitment to God. Even if you receive only an allowance or a little money from a part-time job, it's never too early to develop a habit of tithing. It will help you keep God at the top of your priority list. As you fulfill God's command to meet the needs of others, he will graciously meet—and exceed—your own.

TODAY'S PLAN

How can you develop the discipline of tithing?

GOOD NEWS

TODAY'S PROMISE

How beautiful on the mountains are the feet of the messenger who brings good news, the good news of peace and salvation, the news that the God of Israel reigns!

—ISAIAH 52:7

TODAY'S THOUGHT

The Good News of Jesus the Messiah is that you will find joy and peace when you develop a relationship with him. He came to earth as a human so he could relate to humans. Now he is preparing a place where we will one day live forever with him in peace. The Bible promises an added measure of joy when you share the Good News with others.

TODAY'S PLAN

How can your life be a living testimony of the Good News—the joy and peace you have through a relationship with Jesus?

CELEBRATION

TODAY'S PROMISE

The LORD your God . . . will take delight in you with gladness. . . . He will rejoice over you with joyful songs. —ZEPHANIAH 3:17

TODAY'S THOUGHT

God rejoices and celebrates when his people faithfully follow him and obey his commands. If you trust in him and do what he commands, the almighty God of the universe will celebrate because of you!

TODAY'S PLAN

What is something you can do today that God can celebrate?

HELP

TODAY'S PROMISE

The LORD is my strength and shield. I trust him with all my heart. He helps me, and my heart is filled with joy. I burst out in songs of thanksgiving.

—PSALM 28:7

TODAY'S THOUGHT

If you focus on trying to get yourself out of trouble, you will never see what God wants to do to help you. God loves to help and encourage those who depend on him and trust him completely. When you ask God for help and trust that he will help, you open a lifeline to the God who loves to do the impossible!

TODAY'S PLAN

Do you need help? Are you ready to see what God can do to help you?

JESUS

TODAY'S PROMISE

Christ is the visible image of the invisible God. He existed before anything was created and is supreme over all creation, for through him God created everything in the heavenly realms and on earth. . . . Christ is also the head of the church, which is his body. He is the beginning, supreme over all who rise from the dead. So he is first in everything. . . . [God] made peace with everything in heaven and on earth by means of Christ's blood on the cross. —COLOSSIANS 1:15-20

TODAY'S THOUGHT

These verses give us one of the most powerful descriptions of Jesus in the entire Bible. This Scripture assures you that everything is under the control of Jesus Christ and everything is possible through him. The more you get to know Jesus, the more you will see how he loves and cares for you and the more confident you will be that he keeps his promises.

TODAY'S PLAN

What are you doing to get to know Jesus better?

RISK

TODAY'S PROMISE

Mary responded, "I am the Lord's servant. May everything you have said about me come true." And then the angel left her. —LUKE 1:38

TODAY'S THOUGHT

Take the risk of doing things God's way. When God asks you to follow him, he won't necessarily give you all the information up front. When you step out in faith, he gives you just enough guidance to see where to take the next step. Mary risked her marriage, her reputation, and her future by becoming the mother of Jesus. Following God's will is not without risks, but God promises that it brings the greatest reward.

TODAY'S PLAN

How much risk are you willing to take in following God?

ANGELS

He will order his angels to protect you wherever you go. They will hold you up with their hands so you won't even hurt your foot on a stone. —PSALM 91:11-12

The Bible does not say whether there is one specific "guardian angel" assigned to each believer. It does say that God uses his angels to counsel, guide, protect, minister to, rescue, fight for, and care for his people. Whether he uses one specific angel or a whole host of angels to help you is his choice and your blessing. Chances are that angels have played a greater role in your life than you realize. Thank God today for the supernatural ways he cares for you.

How does knowing that God sends his angels to be involved in your life affect the way you will live today?

GIFTS

A spiritual gift is given to each of us so we can help each other. . . . It is the one and only Spirit who distributes all these gifts. He alone decides which gift each person should have. —1 CORINTHIANS 12:7, 11

TODAY'S THOUGHT

Why do we give gifts? Because gifts are a symbol of our love, commitment, and care for others. When we find the perfect gift for a friend or loved one, it gives us great joy to see that person delight in it. Similarly, God handpicks special gifts for each one of us, and he takes great delight when we use those gifts responsibly and for his glory. Some of his gifts to us are spiritual gifts, unique abilities he gives to each individual.

You never use these spiritual gifts up; rather, the more you use them, the more they grow and help you make a greater contribution to the world around you. They are a symbol of God's deep, personal, and attentive love and commitment to you.

TODAY'S PLAN

What spiritual gift has God given you? How will you use it today?

PEACE

TODAY'S PROMISE

A child is born to us, a son is given to us. The government will rest on his shoulders. And he will be called: Wonderful Counselor, Mighty God, Everlasting Father, Prince of Peace. His government and its peace will never end.

—ISAIAH 9:6-7

TODAY'S THOUGHT

Lasting peace comes only from Jesus Christ, the Prince of Peace. Because he rules over all creation, as well as over your life, you can be sure that one day he will bring complete peace on earth. Until then, he offers you peace of mind and heart when you give him control of your life. You can have peace knowing that your life is in the hands of a loving God who is passionately committed to you.

TODAY'S PLAN

Do you search for peace within yourself or from the Prince of Peace?

DECEMBER 21

CHANGE

TODAY'S PROMISE

God is working in you, giving you the desire and the power to do what pleases him. —PHILIPPIANS 2:13

TODAY'S THOUGHT

God doesn't force change on you. When you invite him into your life, you give him permission to use his power to change you. If you try to change on your own, you won't get good results, but you will get discouraged. Instead, let the very power of God himself begin a work of transformation in you that will last a lifetime. Your life will see dramatic changes if you allow God to do his work in you.

TODAY'S PLAN

How can you allow God to change you from the inside out?

VICTORY

TODAY'S PROMISE

The Mighty One is holy, and he has done great things for me. He shows mercy from generation to generation to all who fear him. His mighty arm has done tremendous things! —LUKE 1:49-51

The Son radiates God's own glory and expresses the very character of God, and he sustains everything by the mighty power of his command. When he had cleansed us from our sins, he sat down in the place of honor at the right hand of the majestic God in heaven. —HEBREWS 1:3

TODAY'S THOUGHT

It's hard to picture the baby Jesus as the mighty God, but he was mighty enough to create the world, live a sinless life, heal countless people, calm storms, and conquer death. He is mighty enough to conquer your troubles, too. Jesus promises to give you ultimate victory!

TODAY'S PLAN

Do you see Jesus only as a meek and lowly baby or as a mighty warrior and victorious Savior?

TIMING OF GOD

TODAY'S PROMISE

When we were utterly helpless, Christ came at just the right time and died for us sinners. —ROMANS 5:6

TODAY'S THOUGHT

God's people had been longing for the Messiah for centuries, yet God sent Jesus to earth at just the right time. We may not fully understand why this was perfect timing until we get to heaven and see God's complete plan. But you can be sure that God sent Jesus at the time when the most people, both present and future, would be reached with the Good News of salvation.

TODAY'S PLAN

How do you see evidence of God's perfect timing in your life?

GIFTS

TODAY'S PROMISE

God loved the world so much that he gave his one and only Son, so that everyone who believes in him will not perish but have eternal life. —JOHN 3:16

TODAY'S THOUGHT

The greatest gift God gives you is his Son. Through his gift of Jesus, he also gives you the gift of eternal life. What makes these gifts so wonderful is that you don't have to work for them or earn them. You simply believe that God has actually given you his Son and the offer of eternal life with him. Then you accept the gifts. And no one can take them away.

TODAY'S PLAN

God has given you gifts too wonderful to keep to yourself. Whom can you share them with?

HUMILITY

TODAY'S PROMISE

The Savior—yes, the Messiah, the Lord—has been born today in Bethlehem, the city of David! And you will recognize him by this sign: You will find a baby wrapped snugly in strips of cloth, lying in a manger.
—LUKE 2:11-12

God blesses those who are humble, for they will inherit the whole earth.
—MATTHEW 5:5

TODAY'S THOUGHT

God often accomplishes his plans in unexpected ways. God chose to have Jesus born in a stable rather than a palace; he chose tiny Bethlehem rather than the capital, Jerusalem; and he chose to proclaim the news of Jesus' birth first to shepherds rather than to kings. Perhaps God did all this to show that life's greatest treasure—salvation through Jesus—is available to all people, no matter what their status.

TODAY'S PLAN

Have you accepted the humble message of salvation that Jesus brings to all people?

CELEBRATION

TODAY'S PROMISE

*[The] festival will be a happy time of celebrating . . .
to honor the Lord your God . . . for it is he who
blesses you with bountiful harvests and gives you
success in all your work.* —DEUTERONOMY 16:14-15

TODAY'S THOUGHT

The Bible teaches that celebration is both
important and necessary. Celebration gives you
the opportunity to experience the joy of hard
work, the satisfaction and rewards of accomplishment, and the good things of creation. It
encourages a spirit of gratitude and renews your
energy for the work yet to be done. Even when a
celebration comes to an end, you can continue
to celebrate the joys of your friends and family
and your relationship with Jesus Christ.

TODAY'S PLAN

*Now that Christmas is over, what can you continue to
celebrate?*

EXAMPLE

TODAY'S PROMISE

I am giving you a new commandment: Love each other. Just as I have loved you, you should love each other. Your love for one another will prove to the world that you are my disciples. —JOHN 13:34-35

TODAY'S THOUGHT

Regardless of the level of your gifts and abilities, God wants you to invest what he's given you into the lives of others. He promises that when you follow his example of love and service, you will become an example to others of Christ's love. Your example will even change the lives of many other people.

TODAY'S PLAN

What can you do today to be an example of Christ's love and service?

WORRY

TODAY'S PROMISE

The LORD keeps watch over you as you come and go, both now and forever. —PSALM 121:8

Don't worry about tomorrow, for tomorrow will bring its own worries. Today's trouble is enough for today. —MATTHEW 6:34

TODAY'S THOUGHT

You can trust God with your future because he is faithful and loves you and promises to guide you to a perfect, eternal future in heaven. Jesus doesn't promise a problem-free life; in fact, he guarantees that life will not be easy. So don't be surprised by hard times, and don't be afraid of them. There is no problem that Jesus can't handle or overcome. Most of the things that you worry might happen never do, so don't waste time worrying. When you're tempted to worry, turn to prayer instead.

TODAY'S PLAN

Make a list of the things you're worrying about today, then give them to God in prayer. He will do what's best for you.

GOALS

TODAY'S PROMISE

*Take delight in the LORD, and he will give you
your heart's desires.* —PSALM 37:4

TODAY'S THOUGHT

As you think about setting goals for the coming
year, here's a place to start: Make a commitment
to learn how to apply your faith to everyday life
and to become more confident about what you
believe. When you pursue these goals, you'll
find that the other priorities in your life will
fall neatly into place because there will be no
conflict between what you believe and what
you do.

TODAY'S PLAN

*Have you ever set goals for your spiritual life before?
Make the extra effort to do so this year.*

FUTURE

TODAY'S PROMISE

The LORD directs our steps, so why try to understand everything along the way?

—PROVERBS 20:24

Humble yourselves before the Lord, and he will lift you up in honor.

—JAMES 4:10

TODAY'S THOUGHT

God reveals just enough of the future to increase your dependence on him. God alone knows everything about the future, and he wants you to be a part of his work in it, so you must rely on him to lead you there. That is the essence of what it means to live by faith. Faith is trusting God to lead you into the future he promises you rather than trying to create your own future by yourself.

TODAY'S PLAN

Are you charting your own future, or are you following God to the future he has for you?

FINISHING WELL

I am certain that God, who began the good work within you, will continue his work until it is finally finished on the day when Christ Jesus returns.

—PHILIPPIANS 1:6

TODAY'S THOUGHT

Another year has slipped by, and you wonder where the time went and how it went so quickly. That's why it is so important to do your best each day, whether in school, in your relation-ships, or in your walk with God. Be faithful to carry out the responsibilities and the calling that God will give you in the new year to come. Then at the end of next year, you will have the satisfac-tion of finishing well and experiencing the pleasure of God.

TODAY'S PLAN

Have you finished well this year? What goals can you set now so that you will finish well next year too?

TOPICAL INDEX

SCRIPTURE INDEX